Camera
with QuarkXPress

A practical guide to creating
direct-to-press documents
on the desktop

Cyndie Klopfenstein

Peachpit Press
Berkeley, California

Camera Ready with QuarkXPress
Cyndie Klopfenstein

Peachpit Press, Inc.
2414 Sixth Street
Berkeley, CA 94710
(800) 283-9444
(510) 548-4393
(510) 548-5991 FAX

Illustrations by Cyndie Klopfenstein
Cover design by Visual Strategies

ISBN 1-56609-089-X

0 9 8 7 6 5 4 3 2 1

Printed and bound in the United States of America.

Dedication

To those who came to learn — and taught me so much:

> Kathy,
> Susan,
> Karen,
> Kathy,
> Donna,
> Shawn,
> Tamara,
> Stephanie,
> Kiki,
> Robert,
> and Cheryl;

To my parents; George and Geraldine, who taught me and I came to learn; and

To my husband, BK, and my son, Coy, who can't be taught and still haven't learned.

Thanx

I know that I nearly put you to sleep with my list in the dedication, but there's been so many that have helped me accumulate enough information to write about.

However, there are also those that helped me get through the writing and editing of this book and I would like to thank them separately.

Don Lohse
Corporate Trainer, Quark, Inc.
Friendly Critic

Nancy McCarthy
Rainwater Press

William Buckingham
President, XChange

Will Whitaker
Vice President Marketing and Sales, XChange

Dorothy Hamner
Proofreader

And thanx to those who gave me something to write about:

Tim Gill
Founder and Chairman, Quark, Inc.

Fred Ebrahimi
President and Chief Executive Officer, Quark, Inc.

Quark's Programmers

XTension Developers

Foreword

When I was asked to write an introduction for *QuarkXPress: Making the Most of Your Negative Experiences*, my first comment was "Can't you change the title?" I hadn't had a chance to actually see the book and had visions of...well, I suppose you can imagine. I was pleasantly surprised. There wasn't a single negative comment about QuarkXPress. In fact, the book provides a wealth of information that is useful to more than just the owners of QuarkXPress.

Quark was started 12 years ago – before the invention of PostScript® and laser printers. We did it on a shoestring budget (about $2000). Every piece of artwork that we produced we did ourselves, usually using press-on letters and hand-inked graphics. This saved us lots of money on "prepress," but we often discovered that the art we had produced was constructed wrongly for the printing press. We would have failed to consider paper wastage or failed to allow room for grippers. We would have to do it all again or, if we were in a hurry, pay to have it reworked. We didn't always save as much money as we should have.

Eventually, of course, we learned to call the printer before we started the art. We learned about printing presses and all their foibles. But it took a long time and we wasted too much time and effort learning. If there had been a single book that talked about proper mechanical layout for common kinds of printed pieces, we would have benefited enormously. If we had had this book, we probably would have saved thousands of dollars.

If you're just getting started in business and are planning to do your own art for standard printed pieces using QuarkXPress, this book will help you eliminate errors and save both time and money. It is an invaluable addition to your library.

Tim Gill
Founder and Chairman Quark, Inc.

*Author's note: After Tim's comment about the title, and then Fred Ebrahimi's (president of Quark, Inc.), and Nancy McCarthy's (my editor), and then Ted Nace's (publisher of Peachpit), I was ready to concede that perhaps it would not be the easiest title to market. However, I'd like to point out that many of the early purchasers bought the book because of the title. To those of you who "got it" and appreciated it — thank you. To those of you who don't (or didn't) — work in this industry long enough and you will.

Preface

After 17 years in print shops, in-house graphics departments, and advertising agencies, I have seen an extraordinarily diverse spectrum of printed pieces — accompanied by equally diverse methods for creating them.

With the advent of desktop technology has come a whole new workforce — people with computer backgrounds rather than people trained in typography or stripping. While it's important to have an understanding of the technology, it's essential for today's desktop publishers to understand the art of printing and pre-press in order to create successful documents.

Camera Ready with QuarkXPress is an attempt to share some of the knowledge that my colleagues and I have acquired over the years. This book will also help the industry's old-timers, trained in the traditional graphic arts, who need to stay on top of the technology while continuing to create high-quality jobs.

The sections of this book are divided into printing processes that share a common feature, such as paper sizes, similar bindery requirements, or the same end use, as with the chapters on cassette and CD jewel case inserts (J-cards).

It is assumed that you have more than a rudimentary knowledge of QuarkXPress and its terminology. But, just in case, keywords and phrases used in the chapter that could be classified as computer-ese or printer's slang appear in bold at first reference within each chapter and are listed alphabetically in the glossary at the back of this guide. Keep in mind that both "languages" may vary from shop to shop, so you'll want to make sure you and your printer or client share the same interpretation of such terms.

If you still need to brush up on your QuarkXPress basics, refer to the "Using QuarkXPress" manual included with the program.

If the instructions require that you use the menus, that location is listed at the bottom of the page and a keyboard equivalent is given if available. An arrow after the menu listing or keyboard equivalent indicates further action such as typing in a value or selecting a file name from a dialog box as with "get text."

I always keep the measurements and tool palettes open when working in QuarkXPress and only open other palettes as required. I mention this because the instructions quite often will send you to one of these two palettes, and it will save you time to keep these open (unless you have a 9" screen, of course).

Much of the content of this guide details procedures for creating sufficient gripper space, crop marks, and registration marks for pre-press and press requirements. Every printer and stripper has idiosyncrasies about these requirements, however, so I highly recommend that you consider the preferences of whomever you're working with. The templates on the disc (Macintosh format included) and the instructions herein will give you a good start.

For the computer wizards out there, communication with your printer is vital. By learning how to make minor adjustments to your files, you will be well on your way to creating truly finished camera-ready documents.

For the typographers, strippers, and printers, I'm convinced you're all deities and can't learn anymore, but I've created this guide just so you'd know what the competition is up to.

Cyndie Klopfenstein

Contents

Section 1

Chapter 1
Crop Marks

rinter's marks tend to be very simple. Many are used interchangeably, even though at one time they had a single purpose. The straight unbroken line, for example, was once used primarily to indicate a **crop** or **trim**, and is now often used to indicate a **perforation** or a **fold**. Though a popular concept, it can be very confusing to a pre-press department that uses a dashed line to indicate a fold or perforation.

For the purposes of this book, an unbroken .25 – .5" (1p6 – 3p) line in **hairline** (.25 pt) width indicates a crop or trim. A dashed line the same width and length indicates a fold or perforation (see illustration below). When using a dashed line, you may want to **call it out** as well. That is, write next to the line that it is a perforation or fold. (I actually draw a text box adjoining the mark and, using 5pt helvetica, type "fold" or "perforation.")

Crop marks at the corners of the page indicate where the **bindery person** should cut (trim) the stock. In the event of a **bleed**, or perhaps when printing several thousand images, a document may be printed on an **oversized sheet** or **several up** on a **parent sheet**. These corner crops will outline the correct **finished size** of each item.

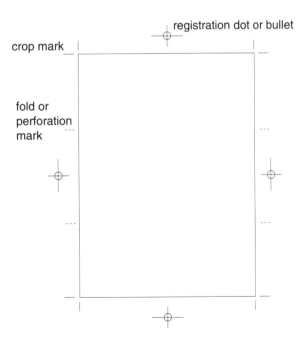

When you **output** to an **imagesetter** and unless you create the QuarkXPress document larger than the actual size, you may need to add additional printer's marks by hand. A .000 **Rapidograph pen** is perfect and marks neatly on **high-resolution output** (**RC paper**), though it does not write well on regular text weight (plain paper) or laser paper.

A **scribing tool** could be used to add marks to **negatives**.

When creating a document such as an 11 X 8.5" tri-fold brochure, make the document size 11.5 X 9". This will allow .25" of extra work area on each edge of the document where you can add fold and perforation marks, rather than having to mark them **traditionally**. You will also need to add corner marks, because the registration marks' **button** in the print **dialog box** will add crop marks at the 11.5 X 9" dimensions.

Some printers also use a mark called the 4" mark. This mark can be included on a document as small as a business card setup. Any job printed on an oversized sheet with a **metal plate** is a candidate for a 4" mark. This mark should be placed on the right-margin edge 4" down from the top **gripper** edge of the sheet. To utilize this mark, you need to know the sheet size that the job is to be printed on in addition to the position of the job on the sheet. Your printer should be able to provide this information.

An extremely **long run**, a multiple-color job, a job being **commercially printed**, or any combination of the three would subject the job to being printed **two or more up**. If the job is to be printed in a multiple format, the printer will determine whether the job will **perfect** (per fekt´ — notice the accent on the second syllable), **work and turn**, or **work and tumble**, and all these processes may make use of the 4" mark to ensure that copy prints in the correct position on the page or that both sides print correctly — exactly 4" from the top of the sheet. This mark also helps align the front to the back.

One other mark is often used with a metal-plated job — a **center mark**. To add this mark, you will need to get the paper size that the job will be printed on from the printer. The center mark will indicate the exact center of the sheet (not the document) and should be placed in the center of the sheet on all four edges.

The 4" mark and the center mark have not been used in any of the instructions of these chapters, but you may choose to add them in anyway.

The right-margin edge of the **press sheet** won't necessarily correspond to the right-margin edge of your document. If for some reason the sheet is printed sideways (**grips** from an edge other than the top), the document's right edge might actually be the bottom, the left, or the top of the **plate**. A single-edged **bleed** is a good reason for a job to grip on an edge other than the top. A **heavy solid** or folds are other reasons.

Printer's marks are usually **dropped in** by the pre-press department of a print shop, and most established departments have these **common marks** already set up for use with a repeated format. I am not recommending that you try to include every type of mark — only to make you aware of the possible additions to, or requirements of, a printed piece.

> **Note:** Three **XTensions**, Crop and Registration Marks, Crop Mark Incase, and PressMarks, enable the user to add crop marks, registration marks, or color bars to a document. You may choose to use these XTensions rather than adding the hand-drawn crop marks as indicated in many of the chapters.

Section 2
A Full Deck

Chapter 2
Business Cards

2-Up Business Cards with 1/4" top gripper trim

Template: BC-8
Document Size:
  3.5 X 4.25"
Finished Size:
  3.5 X 2"

Margins:
T: .25" (1p6)
B: 0
L: 0
R: 0

Facing Pages:
  no
Automatic
Text Box:
  no

Columns:
  1
Gutter Width:

Ruler Guide Positions:

V:

H: 2.25"   (13p6)

Crop/Trim Positions:

V:

H: .25"   (1p6)
      2.25"   (13p6)
both of these are
optional crop marks

Fold Mark Positions:

V:

H:

Recommended
Text Inset:
    .25"   (1p6)

registration marks button

BC-8 6/13/92 11:00 AM Page 8

hand-drawn
trim marks
(optional)

text
box
that
will
step
and
repeat

A

A print shop never prints business cards **1-up**. Most often they are printed **4-up**, but **2-up** is also acceptable. The size of the **press** on which your job will be printed as well as the quantity of your order will determine if you should place four or two cards on each page of your document.

Template BC-8 is 2-up with a .25" (1p6) **trim** from the top card. Paper size is 3.5 X 4.25" and requires only one other trim to separate the two cards. There is no additional trim required from the outside edges, which can be a drawback. Many presses (or press operators) allow ink to collect on this outer edge and the cards may be soiled when packaged for delivery. For this reason, this format is unsuitable for a design that **bleeds**.

> **Tip:** Anywhere that you use a measurement in **points**, simply type a "p" before the number. A "p" appearing after the number will give a **pica** measurement. (For example, p8 = 8 points, 8p = 8 picas. Also 4p2 = 4 picas and 2 points.)

> **Note:** Margins on a business card format should always be .25" (1p6), unless any elements bleed or if the design specifically requires a narrower margin.

Function	Menu Location	Keyboard Equivalent
Open	→ File → Open	Command/O
New	→ File → New	Command/N

To create a business card in this format open template BC-8 or begin a new QuarkXPress document with page dimensions of 3.5 X 4.25".

Margin guides in this case will be .25" (1p6) top, and 0" bottom, left, and right, no facing pages, 1 column, and no automatic text box.

Pull a horizontal **ruler guide** down to the 2.25" (13p6) mark and draw a text box beginning at the top-left page guide intersection to the middle-right page guides; or draw a text box exactly 2" (12p) deep and 3.5" (21p) wide from these same page guides at the top-left edge of the document (0" on the horizontal ruler).

Set text inset to a recommended .25" (1p6) (or as required).

Type the text inside the text box (or get text) and import graphics (get picture) as necessary to complete the design.

Shortcuts/Options

Click on the automatic text box in the new page **dialog box** and once the document opens, click in the text box to make it active and then double click on the W: **field** in the measurements palette. Type in 3.5" (21p) and tab to the H: field (the tab key will automatically highlight this value) and type in 2" (12p). Set text inset to .25" (1p6). The text box is now the appropriate size, and positioned properly for your format.

Function	Menu Location	Keyboard Equivalent
Get Picture	→ File → Get Picture →	Command/E →
Get Text	→ File → Get Text →	Command/E →
Text Inset	→ Item → Modify → Text Inset →	Command/M →

Use the item tool and select all; step and repeat; repeat count: 1, horizontal offset: 0 (zero), and vertical offset: 2" (12p). This will duplicate all elements of the business card and eliminate the need to retype it or to cut, paste, and move.

If **setting** different names in the same design, complete the step and repeat then drag through (or select) the changing text on the second card, and type over with replacement text.

For more than two names, follow the instructions on the previous page and then choose the item tool, select all, and copy. Insert 1 page after page 1 (or as many pages as you will need) scroll to page 2, and paste. Drag items into proper position using the margin guides for alignment. Once again, select the changing text and replace with new text.

Shortcuts/Options

Open a library, choose the item tool, select all, and drag all items into the now open library. Insert page(s) and drag the page layout from the library into position on page 2 (and consecutive pages). Change applicable text.

When you print this document, make sure the registration marks **button** is checked.

Instructions for drawing the crop marks indicating where the .25" (1p6) trim from the top of the card and the center trim are not included here. But, because they are optional, and you may wish to include them, their positioning is shown in the illustration. Printers are aware that this trim is necessary and will do so without these marks.

Function	Menu Location	Keyboard Equivalent
Copy	→ Edit → Copy	Command/C
Go To... (page)	→ Page → Go To... →	Command/J →
Insert (pages)	→ Page → Insert →	
Library	→ Utilities → Library	
Paste	→ Edit → Paste	Command/V
Print	→ File → Print	Command/P
Select All	→ Edit → Select All	Command/A
Step and Repeat	→ Item → Step and Repeat →	Shift/Option/D →

2-Up Business Cards with 1/4" allowance for hand-drawn crops

Template: BC-12

Document Size:
   4 X 4.5"

Finished Size:
   3.5 X 2"

Margins:

T: .25" (1p6)

B: .25" (1p6)

L: .25" (1p6)

R: .25" (1p6)

Facing Pages:
   no

Automatic
Text Box:
   no

Columns:
   1

Gutter Width:

Ruler Guide Positions:

V:

H: 2.25"   (13p6)

Crop/Trim Positions:

V: .25"   (1p6)
       3.75"   (22p6)

H: .25"   (1p6)
       2.25"   (13p6)
       4.25"   (25p6)

Fold Mark Positions:

V:

H:

Recommended
Text Inset:
        .25"   (1p6)

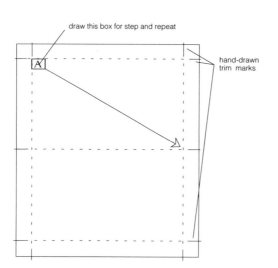

draw this box for step and repeat

hand-drawn
trim marks

A

When your printer requests crop marks on all edges, open template BC-12 or begin a new document 4 X 4.5", with .25" (1p6) margins, no facing pages, 1 column, and no automatic text box.

Pull a ruler guide down to 2.25" (13p6). Draw a text box from the top-left margin guides down to the intersection of the middle-right page guides.

Set text inset as desired, though .25" (1p6) is recommended as it is an adequate gripper edge for most **printing presses**.

Set text (or get text) and add graphics (get picture).

Select the text box and all of its contents with the item tool and step and repeat; repeat count: 1, horizontal offset: 0 (zero), and vertical offset: 2" (12p).

Using the **orthogonal line tool**, add **crop marks** at each corner of the card to indicate **finished size**. A hairline (.25pt) is sufficient **weight** and the crop marks need not be longer than .25" (1p6).

To do this, draw one horizontal crop mark approximately .25" (1p6) long beginning 6pts off the left edge of the document at the .25" (1p6) horizontal margin guide. Extend to within 6pts of the vertical margin guide.

Function	Menu Location	Keyboard Equivalent
Get Picture	→ File → Get Picture	Command/E →
Get Text	→ File → Get Text	Command/E →
New	→ File → New	Command/N
Open	→ File → Open	Command/O
Step and Repeat	→ Item → Step and Repeat	Command/Option/D
Text Inset	→ Item → Modify → Text Inset	Command/M → Text Inset

Keep the crop mark selected, step and repeat; repeat count: 2, horizontal offset: 0 (zero), and vertical offset: 2" (12p). Now select all three crop marks and step and repeat; repeat count: 1, horizontal offset: 3.83" (23p), and vertical offset: 0 (zero).

Repeat this process for the vertical crop marks: Draw the first crop in the upper-left corner, select, step and repeat; repeat count: 1, horizontal offset: 3.5" (21p), and vertical offset: 0 (zero).

Then select both vertical crop marks and step and repeat; repeat count: 1, horizontal offset: 0 (zero), and vertical offset: 4.33" (26p).

> **TIP:** Use your measurements palette to quickly adjust lengths, weights, and positions of crop marks.

> **NOTE: Optronics RIPs** and **imagesetters** require that a **bleed** extend no farther than 1/8" (.125" or p9) off any edge of the sheet.

Function	Menu Location	Keyboard Equivalent
Step and Repeat	→ Item → Step and Repeat →	Command/Option/D →

4-Up Business Cards with 1/4" top gripper trim

Template: BC-16

Document Size:
3.5 X 8.25"

Finished Size:
3.5 X 2"

Margins:

T: .25" (1p6)

B: 0

L: 0

R: 0

Facing Pages:
no

Automatic
Text Box:
no

Columns:
1

Gutter Width:

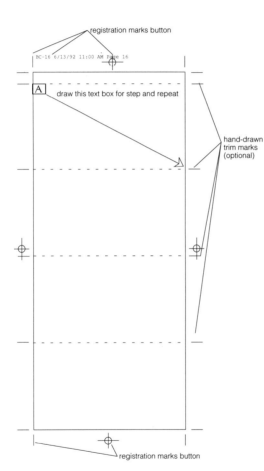

registration marks button

BC-16 6/13/92 11:00 AM Page 16

A draw this text box for step and repeat

hand-drawn
trim marks
(optional)

registration marks button

Ruler Guide Positions:

V:

H: 2.25"   (13p6)

Crop/Trim Positions:

V:

H: .25"   (1p6)
       2.25"   (13p6)
       4.25"   (25p6)
       6.25"   (37p6)
all of these crop marks
are optional

Fold Mark Positions:

V:

H:

Recommended
Text Inset:
        .25"   (1p6)

16

pen template BC-16 or create a new document 3.5 X 8.25". Set page parameters to .25" (1p6) top, and 0" (zero) left, bottom, and right margins; no facing pages, 1 column, and no automatic text box.

Pull a ruler guide down to 2.25" (13p6); draw the text box to fit this area and set the text inset to .25" (1p6) or as desired.

Set all text inside the text box (or get text) and get pictures as required.

Using the item tool, select all, and step and repeat; repeat count: 3, horizontal offset: 0 (zero), and vertical offset: 2" (12p).

Print, making sure the registration marks **button** is checked.

> **Note:** As with the 2-up vertical format it is not necessary to insert a **crop mark** indicating the .25" **trim** from the top or the three cuts to separate the cards. Most printers are aware of the positioning of these **marks** and will make them automatically. (These optional crop marks are shown in the illustration at the left.)

Function	Menu Location	Keyboard Equivalent
Get Picture	→ File → Get Picture	Command/E →
Get Text	→ File → Get Text	Command/E →
New	→ File → New	Command/N
Open	→ File → Open	Command/O
Print	→ File → Print	Command/P →
Select All	→ Edit → Select All	Command/A
Step and Repeat	→ Item → Step and Repeat	Command/Option/D
Text Inset	→ Item → Modify → Text Inset	Command/M → Text Inset

4-Up Business Cards vertical format with 1/4" margin for crops

Template: BC-18

Document Size:
  4 X 8.5"

Finished Size:
  3.5 X 2"

Margins:

T: .25 (1p6)

B: .25 (1p6)

L: .25 (1p6)

R: .25 (1p6)

Facing Pages:
  no

Automatic
Text Box:
  no

Columns:
  1

Gutter Width:

draw this text box for step and repeat

A

hand-
drawn
trim
marks

Ruler Guide Positions:

V:

H: 2.25"   (13p6)

Crop/Trim Positions:

V: .25"   (1p6)

H: .25"   (1p6)
          2.25"   (13p6)
          4.25"   (25p6)
          6.25"   (37p6)
          8.25"   (49p6)

Fold Mark Positions:

V:

H:

Recommended
Text Inset:
        .25"

To create a document that includes **crop marks** on a vertical 4-up format, open template BC-18. Or begin a new 4 X 8.5" page with .25" (1p6) margins on all edges, no facing pages, 1 column, and no automatic text box.

Pull a ruler guide down to 2.25" (13p6) and draw a text box within this set of page guides with a text inset of .25" (1p6) or as required.

Set text (or get text) and import graphics (get picture).

Draw the left, horizontal crop mark beginning 6pts off the edge of the document and extend until 6pts before reaching the .25" (1p6) vertical margin guide. Drawing longer crop marks will place them within the **image area** and cause them to print on the card.

Beginning 6pts to the right of the upper-right vertical margin guide at 3.75" (22p6), draw a second horizontal crop mark to extend 6pts beyond the edge of the document. Choose the item tool, select all, and step and repeat; repeat count: 3, horizontal offset: 0 (zero), and vertical offset: 2" (12p).

Now, select only the bottom two horizontal crop marks and duplicate.

Function	Menu Location	Keyboard Equivalent
Duplicate	→ Item → Duplicate	Command/D
Get Picture	→ File → Get Picture →	Command/E →
Get Text	→ File → Get Text →	Command/E →
New	→ File → New	Command/N
Open	→ File → Open	Command/O
Select All	→ File → Select All	Command/A
Step and Repeat	→ Item → Step and Repeat →	Command/Option/D →
Text Inset	→ Item → Modify → Text Inset	Command/M → Text Inset

NOTE: The duplicate function will retain the parameters last used in the step and repeat **dialog box**. Because of that, the same 2" value used for **stepping all** was retained and implemented during the duplicate.

Finish the document by adding the four vertical crop marks in each corner of the page. Draw the crops individually or draw the first vertical crop in the upper-left-hand corner and (remembering to stay at least 6pts away from the .25" margin guide) step and repeat; repeat count: 1, horizontal offset: 3.5" (21p), and vertical offset: 0 (zero). Select both top vertical crop marks and step and repeat; repeat count: 1, horizontal offset: 0 (zero), and vertical offset: 8.33" (50p).

NOTE: When printing a document that contains crop marks that have been manually added to the document (as described above), you may choose not to implement **registration marks** in the print **dialog box**. This automatic set of marks would indicate page size, not the **final trim size** of the cards. It would include, however, the **header** at the top of the file indicating file name, date, time, page number, and tile position.

Function	Menu Location	Keyboard Equivalent
Step and Repeat	→ Item → Step and Repeat →	Command/Option/D →

4-Up Business Cards with horizontal format that grips from left

Template: BC-22

Document Size:
   7.25 X 4"

Finished Size:
   3.5 X 2"

Margins:

T: 0

B: 0

L: .25" (1p6)

R: 0

Facing Pages:
   no

Automatic
Text Box:
   no

Columns:
   1

Gutter Width:

_____

Ruler Guide Positions:

V: 3.75"   (22p6)

H: 2"   (12p)

_____

Crop/Trim Positions:

V: .25"   (1p6)
       3.75"   (22p6)
both of these crop
marks are optional

H:

_____

Fold Mark Positions:

V:

H:

_____

Recommended
Text Inset:
       .25   (1p6)

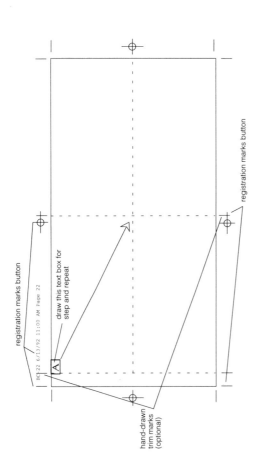

registration marks button

registration marks button

draw this text box for
step and repeat

BC 22 6/13/92 11:00 AM Page 22

A

hand-drawn
trim marks
(optional)

he final two business card templates are **4-up** horizontal formats. The first is with **net cuts** and the second with .5" **gutters**.

Open template BC-22 or begin with a new document 7.25 X 4" with a .25" (1p6) left margin; and 0 (zero) top, bottom, and right margins, no facing pages, 1 column, and no automatic text box.

> **Note:** An extra .25" (1p6) is added to the width (left margin) because this format will **grip from the left**. However, it is unnecessary to indicate this with a **crop mark** because printers are familiar with this format and will automatically make this **cut**. This optional crop mark is shown in the illustration at left.

Pull a ruler guide down to 2" (12p) from the top ruler and vertical ruler guide to 3.75" (22p6). Draw a text box from the upper-left page guides diagonally down to the next intersection.

Text inset should be .25" (1p6) or as desired.

Complete body copy (**set** or get text) and graphics (get picture).

Use the item tool and select all, then step and repeat; repeat count: 1, horizontal offset: 0 (zero), and vertical offset: 2" (12p). Again, select all, then step and repeat; repeat count: 1, horizontal offset: 3.5" (21p), and vertical offset: 0 (zero).

Print with the registration marks **button** on.

Function	Menu Location	Keyboard Equivalent
Get Picture	→ File → Get Picture	Command/E
Get Text	→ File → Get Text	Command/E
New	→ File → New	Command/N
Print	→ File → Print	Command/P
Select All	→ Edit → Select All	Command/A
Step and Repeat	→ Item → Step and Repeat	Command/Option/D
Text Inset	→ Item → Modify → Text Inset	Command/M → Text Inset

4-Up Business Cards with crop marks and gutter allowance

Template: BC-24

Document Size:
 8" X 5"

Finished Size:
 3.5" X 2"

Margins:

T: .25" (1p6)

B: .25" (1p6)

L: .25" (1p6)

R: .25" (1p6)

Facing Pages:
 no

Automatic
Text Box:
 no

Columns:
 2

Gutter Width:
 .5" (3p)

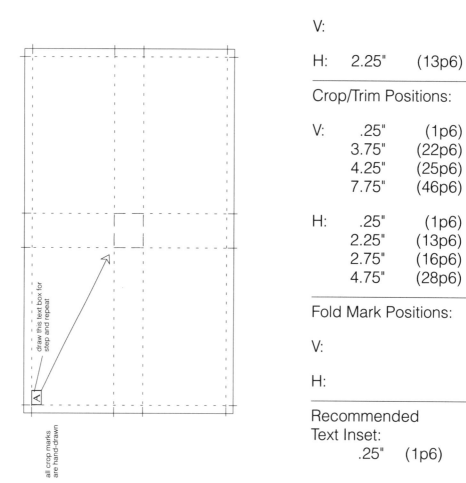

draw this text box for
step and repeat

A

all crop marks
are hand-drawn

Ruler Guide Positions:

V:

H: 2.25"   (13p6)

Crop/Trim Positions:

V: .25"   (1p6)
       3.75"   (22p6)
       4.25"   (25p6)
       7.75"   (46p6)

H: .25"   (1p6)
       2.25"   (13p6)
       2.75"   (16p6)
       4.75"   (28p6)

Fold Mark Positions:

V:

H:

Recommended
Text Inset:
       .25"   (1p6)

Template BC-24, the final template of the business card series, is created with a new document size of 8" X 5". All margin guides are .25" (1p6), no facing pages, 2 columns, .5" (3p) gutter, and no automatic text box.

Pull a horizontal ruler guide down to 2.25" (13p6) and draw a text box with a text inset of .25" (1p6), extending from the top-left margin guide intersection to the middle-right page guide intersection. See illustration.

Set text (or get text) and graphics (get picture) as desired.

Draw a horizontal crop mark aligning on the .25" (1p6) horizontal ruler guide that begins 6pts outside the document edge and extends to the right 6pts before the .25" (1p6) vertical margin guide.

At this same intersection, draw a vertical crop mark. Begin 6pts above the document area and extend down to within 6pts of the .25" (1p6) horizontal margin guide.

Continue in this manner until you have added crop marks to each of the four corners of the first card only.

Using the item tool, select all, and step and repeat; repeat count: 1, horizontal offset: 4" (24p) (an extra .5" to allow for the .5" gutter) and vertical offset: 0 (zero).

Select all, and step and repeat; repeat count: 1, horizontal offset: 0 (zero) and vertical offset: 2.5" (15p).

Function	Menu Location	Keyboard Equivalent
Get Picture	→ File → Get Picture	Command/E →
Get Text	→ File → Get Text	Command/E →
New	→ File → New	Command/N
Select All	→ Edit → Select All	Command/A →
Step and Repeat	→ Item → Step and Repeat →	Command/Option/D →
Text Inset	→ Item → Modify → Text Inset	Command/M → Text Inset

When you have completed **stepping them down**, you may notice that the crop marks overlap each other in the center gutter. This is not a problem, because they will be trimmed away.

Shortcuts/Options

To simplify the process of creating many different versions of the same art, go immediately to the master page, place all common text and graphics (including crop marks). Revert to document view. All common elements now appear as part of the **base art** and only text or graphics that differ from the base must be set (additional names, for example). You can use this shortcut with any of the business card formats. When you insert pages for additional names, the base art will already be there.

Note: This format is generally printed on an 8.5 X 5.5" sheet, centered. There is a **trim** from all four outside edges as well as the center .5" gutter.

Function	Menu Location	Keyboard Equivalent
Document	→ Page → Display → Document	
Master Page	→ Page → Display → Master Page	

Tip: You can **set** vertical cards using any of the formats discussed in this chapter. Begin with a small text box, rotate it 90° and then stretch it to fit in the page guides you have drawn for your chosen format.

All graphics that are imported will also need to be rotated 90°. It is easiest to enter this value in the measurements palette once the item(s) have been selected. Rotate one completed card, ensure that its position is correct, then step and repeat.

Note: Rotations will not affect your step and repeats or any other process discussed in this chapter.

Note: On occasion you will need to create business cards with less than .25" (1p6) margins. Using the **XTension** SetInset, you could even set all four margins at different values. However, keep in mind that cutting cards apart is an unprecise art and running copy closer than .25" (1p6) to an edge that will be trimmed is risky.

Function	Menu Location	Keyboard Equivalent
Rotate	→ Item → Modify → Box Angle	Command/M →
Step and Repeat	→ Item → Step and Repeat →	Command/Option/D →

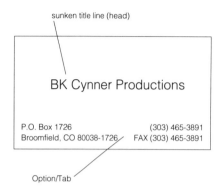

sunken title line (head)

BK Cynner Productions

P.O. Box 1726   (303) 465-3891
Broomfield, CO 80038-1726   FAX (303) 465-3891

Option/Tab

Shortcuts/Options

A great shortcut for **sinking** the title line or first line of a business card (or any other document for that matter) is to use the first baseline offset in the modify dialog box of the item menu. A value entered here will drop the first baseline (measuring from the top of the text box) by that value. A first baseline offset must be a larger value than the current type size for this to have an effect.

Another commonly used function is setting text flush left and flush right, especially when the design calls for the address to flush to the left corner and the phone and FAX number to flush to the right. See the illustration above.

In QuarkXPress 3.11, simply press the tab key while holding down the option key. Text appearing after the tab key will flush to the right-most margin.

In QuarkXPress 3.0, setting your text with the tab in place as though you had set a right-margin tab and then selecting your text and choosing right alignment will achieve the same effect.

Function	**Menu Location**	**Keyboard Equivalent**
Right (alignment)	→ Style → Alignment → Right	Command/Shift/R
Modify	→ Item → Modify →	Command/M → First Baseline Offset

Section 2
A Full Deck

Chapter 3
Rolodex® Cards

Rolodex Cards 2-Up floating (centered) on a 5.5 X 8.5" sheet

Template: RC-30

Document Size:
  5.5 X 8.5"

Finished Size:
  4 X 2.5"

Margins:

T: .75" (4p6)

B: .75" (4p6)

L: .75" (4p6)

R: .75" (4p6)

Facing Pages:
  no

Automatic
Text Box:
  no

Columns:
  1

Gutter Width:

Ruler Guide Positions:

V:

H: 6p5
      15p6

Crop/Trim Positions:

V: 4p6
      28p6

H: 4p6
      34p6

Fold Mark Positions:

V:

H:

Recommended
Text Inset:
      ascending tab: p3
      card area: p6

draw these two text boxes
to fit within the guidelines
then step and repeat and rotate

this trim mark indicates
the width of the tab

all crop and
trim marks are
hand-drawn
in place

this trim mark
indicates the
depth of the tab

slotted area, unusable

once rotated, align to these
page guides as shown

Even though they must be **die cut**, **Rolodex cards** are as simple as a business card. The template RC-30, a **2-up** Rolodex card format, seems at first to waste paper. This may be true, but because the card must be **die cut,** the paper size should not be under 5.5 X 8.5", and the cards should be centered on the sheet. This gives the **die cutter** plenty of **gripper space** and **trim allowance**.

Because **crop marks** are included in this setup, your **engraver** should not have any problems aligning the card to the **die**.

> **Note:** This template has been created using **picas**; therefore, all measurements are given in picas only. I find them easier to use when creating a document like this. You can change this setting in the ***preferences* dialog box**.

Begin with a new document 5.5 X 8.5", with .75" (4p6) margins, no facing pages, 1 column, and no automatic text box.

Pull horizontal ruler guides down to 6p5 (the bottom of the **tab**) and 15p6 (the bottom of usable text space — below this there will be slots for fitting the card into a holder).

Draw a short text box beginning at the top margin guide and extend it down and across to the ruler guide at 6p5. This is the area for your tab, and because tabs are of varying widths, you will need to set your text/graphics (or get text/get picture) to fit the width of your chosen tab size.

Function	Menu Location	Keyboard Equivalent
Get Picture	→ File → Get Picture →	Command/E →
Get Text	→ File → Get Text →	Command/E →
New	→ File → New	Command/N
Open	→ File → Open	Command/O
Ruler Increments	→ Edit → Preferences → General → Horizontal/Vertical Measure →	Command/Y →

Be sure to keep text and/or graphics at least 3pts away from the top and left **trims** and about the same amount from the ruler guide at 6p5. If you allow this copy to drop down any farther, it may be hidden by the card in front of it when in its Rolodex file.

Draw another text box beginning at the 6p5 ruler guide and extend it down to the 15p6 ruler guide. Set the text inset to p6 (or as desired) to keep the copy from running too close to a **die-cut edge** and set all text and graphics.

Using the orthogonal line tool, draw a horizontal crop mark on each outside edge aligned with the 4p6 horizontal margin guide. Extend it no closer than 6pts to outside margin guides. Select both marks and step and repeat; repeat count: 1, horizontal offset: 0 (zero), and vertical offset: 15p.

Draw a vertical crop mark at the upper-left margin guides and extend down to within 6pts of the tab text box. Select this crop mark, step and repeat; repeat count: 1, horizontal offset: 24p, and vertical offset: 0 (zero). Draw another vertical crop to indicate the width of the tab.

Draw an additional horizontal crop mark aligned on the 6p5 horizontal ruler guide on the side opposite the tab. This indicates the bottom of the tab area and the top of the card.

Select all; group, duplicate, and rotate 180°. Drag downward into position so that the top of the tab text box aligns with the 46p6 margin guide.

Print without registration marks, as you have already drawn them in.

Function	Menu Location	Keyboard Equivalent
Duplicate	→ Item → Duplicate	Command/D
Print	→ File → Print	Command/P
Rotate	→ Item → Modify → Box Angle	Command/M →
Select All	→ Edit → Select All	Command/A
Step and Repeat	→ Item → Step and Repeat	Command/Shift/D
Text Inset	→ Item → Modify → Text Inset	Command/M →

Section 2
A Full Deck

Chapter 4
Postcards

Postcards have parameters set forth by the United States Postal Service (USPS) regarding minimum and maximum size, minimum and maximum weight, and even a few about text content and placement. You will also want to keep in mind efficient printing sizes, which may be affected by colors and quantity.

I have included only two **templates** (**net cut** and **oversized pages** with margin allowance for crop marks) for each of the two most common sizes of **postcards**. These templates may be combined with the templates for the **business reply mail post card** templates, which provide USPS-approved copy and format for a postcard to be returned to the addressee.

The first two templates contain text for a 5.5 X 4.25" postcard placed **4-up** on an 11 X 8.5" and an 12 X 9.5". The second two templates are for a 5 X 3.5" postcard placed **6-up** in an 14 X 8.5" and an oversized 14 X 19" document. All of these postcards have a built-in .25" margin instead of a text inset. Also, while text and graphics can extend outside these lines, it is not recommended.

Any card within the dimensions and weight requirements in Appendix 2 can be mailed at the **postcard rate**. It is always best to have your printer cut down a sheet of your chosen **stock** to the **finished size** and have its weight and size pre-approved at the local post office.

4-Up Postcard, horizontal or vertical format, net cut 8.5 X 11"

Template: PC-36
or PC-37 (vertical)

Document Size:
    11 X 8.5"
or letter

Finished Size:
    5.5 X 4.25"
or 4.25 X 5.5"

Margins:

T: 0

B: 0

L: 0

R: 0

Facing Pages:
    no

Automatic
Text Box:
    yes

Columns:
    1

Gutter Width:

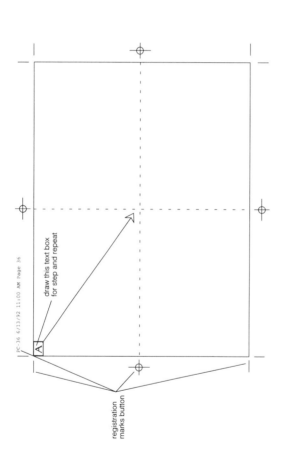

Ruler Guide Positions:

V:

H:

Crop/Trim Positions:

V:

H:

Fold Mark Positions:

V:

H:

Recommended
Text Inset:
    .25"

To create a horizontal 11 X 8.5" 4-up **postcard** format, begin a new document with 0" (zero) margins, no facing pages, 1 column, and click on the automatic text box. Or open template PC-36.

Activate the text box and, using the measurements palette, double click in the W: **field** of the measurements palette: type in 5.5" (33p) and tab to the H: field (the value is highlighted); type in 4.25" (25p6). The enter or return key will apply these values.

Set all text (or get text) and graphics (get picture) and add a text inset of .25"(1p6).

Using the item tool, select all elements of this card and step and repeat; repeat count: 1, horizontal offset: 5.5" (33p), and vertical offset: 0 (zero).

Select all elements of both cards, step and repeat; repeat count: 1, horizontal offset: 0 (zero), and vertical offset: 4.25" (25p6).

For a vertical postcard (template PC-36) of the same dimensions, begin with a letter-size document. All other parameters should be the same, except the dimensions for the text box will be W: 4.25" (25p6) and H: 5.5" (33p).

Select all elements of the postcard and step and repeat; repeat count: 1, horizontal offset: 4.25" (25p6), and vertical offset: 0 (zero). Select both postcards, step and repeat; repeat count: 1, horizontal offset: 0 (zero), and vertical offset: 5.5" (33p).

Print with the registration marks **button** on.

Function	Menu Location	Keyboard Equivalent
Get Text	→ File → Get Text →	Command/E →
Get Picture	→ File → Get Picture →	Command/E →
New	→ File → New	Command/N
Open	→ File → Open	Command/O
Print	→ File → Print	Command/P
Select All	→ Edit → Select All	Command/A
Step and Repeat	→ Item → Step and Repeat →	Command/Option/D →
Text Inset	→ Item → Modify → Text Inset	Command/M →

4-Up Postcard with allowance for hand-drawn crop marks

Template: PC-38
or PC-39 (vertical)

Document Size:
  12 X 9.5"
or 9.5 X 12"

Finished Size:
  5.5 X 4.25"
or 4.25 X 5.5"

Margins:

T: .25" (1p6)

B: .25" (1p6)

L: .25" (1p6)

R: .25" (1p6)

Facing Pages:
  no

Automatic
Text Box:
  yes

Columns:
  1

Gutter Width:

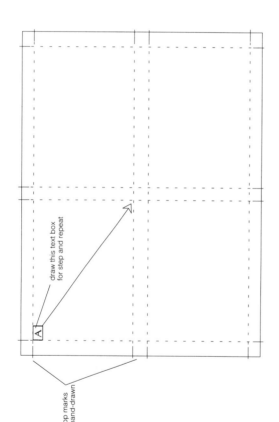

draw this text box
for step and repeat

A

all crop marks
are hand-drawn

Ruler Guide Positions:

V:

H:

Crop/Trim Positions:

V:	.25"	(1p6)
	5.75"	(34p6)
	6.25"	(37p6)
	11.75"	(70p6)

H:	.25"	(1p6)
	4.5"	(27p)
	5"	(30p)
	9.25"	(55p6)

Fold Mark Positions:

V:

H:

Recommended
Text Inset:
  .25" (1p6)

Open template PC-38 for an **oversized document** with **center trims** and allowance for **crop marks** outside the **image area**. Use this format if the postcard has items that **bleed**. The new document is 12 X 9.5", .25" (1p6) margins for all edges, no facing pages, 1 column, and click on the automatic text box.

Activate the text box and double click on the W: **field** of the measurements palette, type 5.5" (33p) tab to the H: field, and type 4.25" (25p6). The enter or return key will apply these values.

Set text (or get text) and graphics (get picture). Text inset is .25" (1p6) or as desired.

Option-click on the orthogonal line tool and draw vertical and horizontal crop marks (no longer than .25" [1p6]) at each corner of the text box. Select all and step and repeat; repeat count: 1, horizontal offset: 6" (36p), and vertical offset: 0" (zero).

Select all, step and repeat; repeat count: 1, horizontal offset: 0 (zero), and vertical offset: 4.75" (28p6). The crop marks at the center gutters will overlap. If you did not draw crop marks longer than .25", they will stay within the .5" gutter.

For a vertical format; open template PC-39 or a new 9.5 X 12" document and follow the steps above until you get to the step and repeat. Then: select all and step and repeat; repeat count: 1, horizontal offset: 4.75" (28p6), and vertical offset: 0" (zero).

Select all, step and repeat; repeat count: 1, horizontal offset: 0 (zero), and vertical offset: 6" (36p).

Function	Menu Location	Keyboard Equivalent
Get Text	→ File → Get Text	Command/E
Get Picture	→ File → Get Picture	Command/E
New	→ File → New	Command/N
Open	→ File → Open	Command/O
Select All	→ Edit → Select All	Command/A
Step and Repeat	→ Item → Step and Repeat	Command/Option/D
Text Inset	→ Item → Modify → Text Inset	Command/M →

6-Up Postcard (minimum allowable size)

Template PC-40
Document Size:
  8.5 X 14"
Finished Size:
  5 X 3.5"

Margins:
T: 0
B: 0
L: 0
R: 0

Facing Pages:
  no
Automatic
Text Box:
  yes

Columns:
  1

Gutter Width:

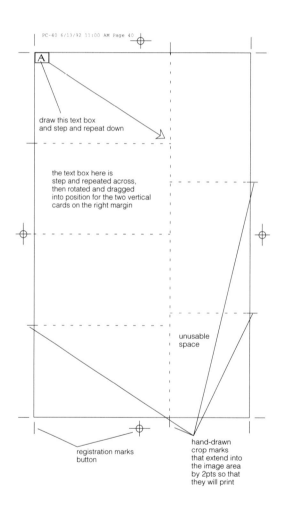

PC-40 6/13/92 11:00 AM Page 40

A

draw this text box
and step and repeat down

the text box here is
step and repeated across,
then rotated and dragged
into position for the two vertical
cards on the right margin

unusable
space

registration marks
button

hand-drawn
crop marks
that extend into
the image area
by 2pts so that
they will print

Ruler Guide Positions:

V:

H:

Crop/Trim Positions:

V: 5"   (30p)

left edge:
H: 3.5"   (21p)
       7"   (42p)
       10.5"   (63p)

right edge:
H: 5"   (21p)
       10"   (42p)

Fold Mark Positions:

V:

H:

Minimum
Text Inset:
       .25"
(no less, as this amount is also
used as gripper space for the
press. Because of this, this
format is unsuitable for
postcards that bleed.)

Template PC-40 houses six 3.5 X 5" **postcards** and was created with a document size of 8 X 14", 0" (zero) margins, no facing pages, 1 column, and an automatic text box.

Activate the text box and double click the value listed in the W: **field**; type 5" (30p) and tab to the H: field; type 3.5" (21p). The enter or return key will apply these values.

Set all text (or get text) and graphics (get picture) with a recommended text inset of no less than .25" (1p6) and select all elements. Step and repeat; repeat count: 3, horizontal offset: 0 (zero), and vertical offset: 3.5" (21p).

Select all elements of the second postcard only and step and repeat; repeat count: 1, horizontal offset: 5" (30p), and vertical offset: 0 (zero). Without releasing the selection, double-click the rotation value in the measurements palette (this should currently be 0°) and change it to -90°. Choose the item tool and drag this selected postcard (a step and repeat will hold the selection of the item once it has been created) to the upper-right margin guides.

Again, without releasing the selection, step and repeat; repeat count: 1, horizontal offset: 0 (zero), and vertical offset: 5" (30p).

Function	Menu Location	Keyboard Equivalent
Get Picture	→ File → Get Picture →	Command/E →
Get Text	→ File → Get Text →	Command/E →
New	→ File → New	Command/N
Select All	→ Edit → Select All	Command/A
Step and Repeat	→ Item → Step and Repeat →	Command/Option/D →
Text Inset	→ Item → Modify → Text Inset	Command/M →
Rotate	→ Item → Modify → Box Angle	Command/M →

Note: This document should include **crop marks** and requires that they extend into the **image area** by at least 2pts. Instruct the printer or film stripper to **opaque** this portion out. QuarkXPress will not print items appearing solely in the pasteboard area, so by extending these crops into the image area (even by the smallest amount) you ensure that they print. However, the printable image area of your **output device** must, of course, be larger than 8.5 X 14", as it is on most **high-resolution printers**.

Add horizontal and vertical crop marks .25" (1p6) long and extending into the document 2pts at the intersection of each of the postcards (see note above) as seen in the illustration at the beginning of this description.

The rotated postcards will have an outside horizontal crop mark at 5" (30p) and at 10" (60p).

Print with the registration marks **button** on.

Function	Menu Location	Keyboard Equivalent
Print	→ File → Print	Command/P

6-Up Postcard with 1/4" allowance for hand-drawn crop marks

Template PC-44

Document Size:
9 X 14.5"

Finished Size:
5 X 3.5"

Margins:

T: .25 (1p6)

B: .25 (1p6)

L: .25 (1p6)

R: .25 (1p6)

Facing Pages:
no

Automatic
Text Box:
yes

Columns:
1

Gutter Width:

Ruler Guide Positions:

V:

H:

Crop/Trim Positions:

V: .25"   (1p6)
       5.25"   (31p6)
       8.75"   (52p6)

H:
left margin
       .25"   (1p6)
       3.75"   (22p6)
       7.25"   (43p6)
       10.75"   (64p6)
       14.25"   (85p6)

right margin
       .25"   (1p6)
       5.25"   (31p6)
       10.25"   (61p6)

Recommended
Text Inset:
       .25" (1p6)

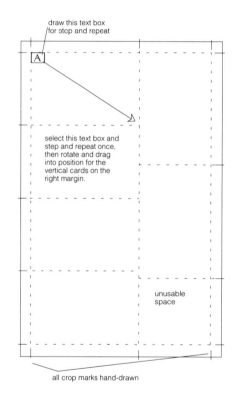

draw this text box for step and repeat

A

select this text box and step and repeat once, then rotate and drag into position for the vertical cards on the right margin.

unusable space

all crop marks hand-drawn

he last **postcard** format is **6-up** with .25" (1p6) extra margin allowance on all edges for hand-drawn **crop marks**.

Open template PC-44 or begin a new 9 X 14.5" document, .25" (1p6) margins, no facing pages, 1 column, and click on the automatic text box.

Activate the automatic text box and double click on the W: **field** of the measurements palette, type 5" (30p), tab to the H: field and type 3.5" (21p).

Set text inset to a recommended .25" (1p6) or as desired and add the text (or get text) and graphics (get picture).

Select the postcard and its contents, and step and repeat; repeat count: 1, horizontal offset: 8" (48p), and vertical offset: 0 (zero). **Holding the selection** of the second card only (or reselecting this card and its contents), rotate -90° and move the card to align with the margin guides in the upper-right corner.

Option-select the orthogonal line tool and, in the upper-left corner, begin 6pts off the document edge and draw a vertical crop mark on the .25" margin guide extending down 6pts before the .25" horizontal margin guide. Now draw a horizontal crop mark at the same corner and in the same manner, stopping 6pts before the .25" vertical margin guide. See the illustration at left.

Select the top-left postcard, its items, and the horizontal crop mark only. Step and repeat; repeat count: 3, horizontal offset: 0 (zero), and vertical offset: 3.5" (21p).

Function	Menu Location	Keyboard Equivalent
Get Text	→ File → Get Text →	Command/E →
Get Picture	→ File → Get Picture →	Command/E →
New	→ File → New	Command/N
Open	→ File → Open	Command/O
Step and Repeat	→ Item → Step and Repeat →	Command/Option/D →
Text Inset	→ Item → Modify → Text Inset →	Command/M →
Rotate	→ Item → Modify → Box Angle →	Command/M →

Select the last horizontal crop mark only, duplicate. Draw a .25" (1p6) vertical crop mark below the last postcard on the .25" vertical margin guide, no closer than 6pts to the bottom of the text box.

Select the top and bottom vertical crop marks on the left .25" vertical margin guide, step and repeat; repeat count: 1, horizontal offset: 5" (30p), and vertical offset: 0 (zero).

Select the two vertical crop marks at the 5.25" horizontal ruler mark (near the center of the sheet) and step and repeat; repeat count: 1, horizontal offset 3.5" (21p), and vertical offset 0 (zero).

To finish, begin 6pts to the right of the top-right corner of the top rotated text box and draw a horizontal crop mark and extend 6pts off the edge of the document.

Select the rotated postcard, its contents, and the horizontal crop mark, step and repeat; repeat count: 1, horizontal offset: 0 (zero), and vertical offset: 5" (30p). Select the new horizontal crop mark only and duplicate.

Print, without the registration marks **button** on.

Function	Menu Location	Keyboard Equivalent
Duplicate	→ Item → Duplicate	Command/D
Print	→ File → Print	Command/P
Step and Repeat	→ Item → Step and Repeat →	Command/Option/D →

Section 2
A Full Deck

Chapter 5
Business Reply Mail Postcard

Business reply mail (BRM) postcards are governed by the same restrictions as a **postcard**. The only difference is that the text instructs the post office to return the mail to the addressee and that the postage will be paid by same. Because these cards are read by a postal service computer, each element must be in precisely the correct position.

See the illustration on page 50 for an example of text placement.

> **Note:** Return the order form from the back of this book to receive a clear-film guide that helps you correctly place the elements in a BRM postcard.

> **Note:** Refer to Chapter 3: Postcards, for information on how to set text for the back of a BRM postcard.

The measurements in this document all appear in picas. You can change your ruler increments to picas in the preferences → general dialog box.

Function	Menu Location	Keyboard Equivalent
Ruler Increments	→ Edit → Preferences → General → Horizontal/Vertical Measure →	Command/Y →

4-Up Business Reply Mail Card

Template BRM-50

Document Size:
11 X 8.5"

Finished Size:
5.5 X 4.25"

Margins:

T: 0

B: 0

L: 0

R: 0

Facing Pages:
no

Automatic
Text Box:
no

Columns:
1

Gutter Width:

Ruler Guide Positions:

V: 9p
    14p
    31p

H: p2
    4p3
    23p3
    23p8
    24p
    25p6

Crop/Trim Positions:

V:

H:

Fold Mark Positions:

V:

H:

Recommended
Text Inset:

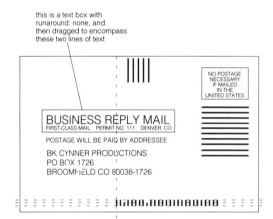

this is a text box with
runaround: none, and
then dragged to encompass
these two lines of text

BUSINESS REPLY MAIL
FIRST-CLASS MAIL   PERMIT NO. 111   DENVER, CO

POSTAGE WILL BE PAID BY ADDRESSEE

BK CYNNER PRODUCTIONS
PO BOX 1726
BROOMFIELD CO 80038-1726

NO POSTAGE
NECESSARY
IF MAILED
IN THE
UNITED STATES

o create a 5.5 X 4.25" **business reply mail postcard**, open template BRM-50 or start a new 11 X 8.5" document with 0" (zero) margins, no facing pages, 1 column, and click on the automatic text box.

Change the horizontal and vertical ruler increments to **picas**.

Pull horizontal ruler guides down from the top ruler to 23p3, 23p8, 24p, and 25p6. Pull a vertical ruler guide to 9p. These ruler guides mark the area in which your **bar code** must fall. Also, the bar code must contain 22 to 24 bars per inch. If you use these ruler guides, you will stay safely within this range.

The first horizontal ruler guide (at 23p3) indicates the height of the taller bars of the code. The second (at 23p8) the height of the shorter bars, and the third (at 24p) shows the bottom of the bar code. The last horizontal ruler guide marks the **trim edge** of the postcard.

Begin at the 9p vertical ruler guide and draw a 1pt rule from the 23p3 horizontal ruler guide down to the 24p horizontal ruler guide. Select this rule and step and repeat; repeat count: 51, horizontal offset: 3pts, and vertical offset: 0 (zero).

Next, refer to your designated BRM postcard instructional sheet (you can get this from the post office) and, for those bars that need to be short, drag the top handle to the second ruler guide.

Function	Menu Location	Keyboard Equivalent
New	→ File → New	Command/N
Open	→ File → Open	Command/O
Step and Repeat	→ Item → Step and Repeat →	Command/Option/D →

Option-click on the rulers to remove all ruler guides. Ensure that the actual page area (not pasteboard) is touching both the top and the left rulers (go to: 1), and option-click on both rulers to remove all ruler guides.

Pull a new vertical ruler guide from the left ruler to 31p6 and a horizontal ruler guide to 1p6. Draw a text box 6p X 5p (or draw a small text box and type 6p and 5p in the W: and H: **fields** of the measurements palette).

Select the content tool, click inside this text box and type (in 8pt Helvetica):

NO POSTAGE
NECESSARY
IF MAILED
IN THE
UNITED STATES

Be sure to use these exact **line breaks** and **all caps**.

With the content tool still inside this text box, select all and center horizontally and vertically (vertical alignment) and set text inset to 3pts.

Use the item tool to align the text box with the upper-right page guides.

Frame the text box with a hairline (.25pt) or .5pt frame.

Function	**Menu Location**	**Keyboard Equivalent**
Centered (Alignment)	→ Style → Alignment → Centered	Command/Shift/C
Frame	→ Item → Frame	Command/B
Go To... (pages)	→ Page → Go To...	Command/J →
Remove Ruler guides		Option/click on ruler
Select All	→ Edit → Select All	Command/A
Text Inset	→ Item → Modify → Text Inset	Command/M →
Vertical (alignment)	→ Item → Modify → Alignment → Vertical	Command/M →

Draw a 2.5pts horizontal rule, 6 picas wide and 9pts below this text box. This rule should be flush with the right ruler guide at 31p6.

Draw a second text box beginning 6 picas from the left edge of the card and 10 picas down (you may wish to pull ruler guides out first) and extend the text box to within 3 picas of the postage text box and horizontal rule.

Set the following text in all caps (inserting custom text where required):
        BUSINESS REPLY MAIL
        FIRST-CLASS MAIL (tab) PERMIT NO. (XXX) (tab) CITY, STATE
        POSTAGE WILL BE PAID BY ADDRESSEE
        COMPANY NAME
        STREET ADDRESS
        CITY STATE ZIP

Do not kern or track the text because it may become illegible to the postal service's computer scanners. You can vertically space (leading) as desired but be sure to add 1p extra paragraph space before the "postage will be paid by addressee" and the "company name" lines. The text should not be smaller than 8pt. The words "Business Reply Mail" must be in 20pt or larger text. You are permitted to horizontally scale this line of text to fit it within this text box.

Because you have used the tab key between the clusters of type on the First-Class Mail line, select this line (or simply insert your cursor in this line) and go to the tabs dialog box. **Set a center tab** in the center of the text box and a right tab at the right margin. Click apply to ensure that there is equal space between these three blocks of text. Adjust.

Function	Menu Location	Keyboard Equivalent
Horizontal Scale	→ Style → Horizontal Scale →	Command/ [or Command/]
Leading	→ Style → Leading	Command/Shift/E →
Space Before	→ Style → Formats → Space Before	Command/Shift/F →
Tab	→ Style → Tabs	Command/Shift/T →

Note: As long as you remain within the constraints from each edge, you have a small amount of leeway here — it's more important that this "look" correct than that the tab is exactly in the center of the box. Therefore, adjusting it visually is better than mechanically.

Shortcut/Option:

Use the **XTension** InsertSpace to evenly distribute this line of text. To do this, select the line of text and choose InsertSpace from the Utilities menu.

Pull a horizontal ruler guide to align with the **baseline** of the company name, then select the 2.5pt rule below the postage text box. Step and repeat this rule down as many times as necessary so that the last rule closely aligns with the baseline of the company name. Repeat count: (as necessary), horizontal offset: 0 (zero), and vertical offset: 9pts.

Adjust the leading in the company name so that it lines up with the closest horizontal rule. Duplicate rules or adjust leading as necessary.

Draw one more text box 16p X 3p (you may need to adjust this size to fit your type), frame it with a .5pt rule, and set its runaround to none. Select the item tool, click on and drag the text box over the lines: "Business Reply Mail" and "First-Class Mail." (See illustration on the previous page.) Adjust this text box to encompass these two lines — but do not touch any of the text around it or on either side. It 's okay to allow this box to move to within 1p6 of the bars on the right.

Function	Menu Location	Keyboard Equivalent
Duplicate	→ Item → Duplicate	Command/D
Frame	→ Item → Frame →	Command/B →
Leading	→ Style → Leading →	Command/E →
Runaround	→ Item → Runaround →	Command/T →
Step and Repeat	→ Item → Step and Repeat →	Command/Shift/D →

To finish this postcard, you must add your personalized **FIM**. To do this, remove all ruler guides. Pull a new vertical ruler guide to 14p and horizontal ruler guides to 2pts and 4p3. Draw a 2pt vertical rule beginning at the 2pts horizontal ruler guide and extending down to the 4p3 ruler guide (lining up with the vertical ruler guide at 14p).

Select the rule, and step and repeat; repeat count: 8, horizontal offset: p4.5, and vertical offset: 0 (zero). Delete those bars not used in your FIM.

To make the document **4-up**, select all and step and repeat; repeat count: 1, horizontal offset: 5.5" (33p), and vertical offset: 0 (zero).

Select all and step and repeat; repeat count: 1, horizontal offset: 0 (zero), and vertical offset: 4.25" (25p6).

To create a BRM postcard for the 3.5 X 5" postcard format, use the instructions listed here and adjust the measurements as necessary to accommodate the smaller size. Follow these instructions and use your clear-film guide to ensure proper placement.

Print, with the registration marks **button** on.

Function	Menu Location	Keyboard Equivalent
Print	→ File → Print	Command/P →
Select All	→ Edit → Select All	Command/A
Step and Repeat	→ Item → Step and Repeat →	Command/Shift/D →

Section 3
You've Been Invited

Chapter 6
Baronial Cards

Baronial cards are often used for invitations, announcements, or note cards. These **beveled-edge** cards come in a flat format or one that is **pre-scored** for folding. They are classified by size, such as A-2 or A-6 (flat or when folded). All baronials have a corresponding envelope size (A-2 envelope, A-6 envelope, etc.). See Appendix 3 for sizes.

To create a non-folded baronial card, create a new document to match the card size (flat in the case of a non-foldable card and folded down for a **scored** card). There are no templates for this format.

The beveled edge is .5" wide and you must allow additional space inside of this bevel as a margin (.25" [1p6] is suggested). Therefore, the margins should be set to .75" (4p6), no facing pages, 1 column, and click on the automatic text box.

Once the text has been **set** inside the existing text box (or get text), adjust the vertical alignment for aesthetic appeal — centered is usually the desired effect. For **script text**, use generous leading as well as a large type size to improve legibility.

Function	Menu Location	Keyboard Equivalent
Centered	→ Style → Alignment → Centered	Command/Shift/ C
Get Text	→ File → Get Text →	Command/E →
Leading	→ Style → Leading →	Command/Shift/E →
New	→ File → New	Command/N
Size	→ Style → Size →	Command/Shift/ \ →
Vertical (alignment)	→ Item → Modify → Alignment → Vertical	Command/M →

To create the folded baronial, begin in the same manner (be sure that your new document is the same as the size of the card folded down) and click on the facing pages **button** in the new page **dialog box**.

>**Note:** This method will only work correctly with a **vertical format**.

Set text (or get text) and insert 3 pages after page 1. Each page indicates a **panel** on the card and all margins should match. (The **inside back panel** [unbeveled] can have a narrower margin, however, as there is no bevel.) Type can appear on the **inside front panel** but here again, the margins should be .75" as the bevel is still present — just **embossed** in the opposite direction.

For a flat **horizontal format**, use the method on the previous page for the flat card and create the document page size to match that of your horizontal baronial card. Insert pages to represent each panel and continue as directed.

Function	Menu Location	Keyboard Equivalent
Get Text	→ File → Get Text	Command/E →
Insert (pages)	→ Page → Insert	
New	→ File → New	Command/N

For a folded, horizontal baronial, use the method on page 59, but rotate all items 90°.

Create a new document as vertical rather than horizontal (just transpose the dimensions). Turn on facing pages, but no automatic text box.

Once open, draw a small text box and rotate 90°. Stretch the text box to fit within the margin guides.

Type all text (or get text) and add graphics (get picture). (Don't forget to rotate the graphics, too.)

Insert 1 page per panel. If the panel on page 2 (**inside front panel**) is blank, it will still need a page. You will not need a page for the **outside back panel** if it is blank.

Click on the spreads button when printing. This will join the inside front and inside back panels (pages) as one, with the **registration dot** (**bullet**) indicating the center fold. It will not be necessary to add a **fold mark** between the two pages.

Function	Menu Location	Keyboard Equivalent
Get Picture	→ File → Get Picture →	Command/E →
Get Text	→ File → Get Text →	Command/E →
Insert (pages)	→ Page → Insert	
Print	→ File → Print	Command/P →
Rotate	→ Item → Modify → Box Angle →	Command/M →

Section 3
You've Been Invited

Chapter 7
Stock Invitations

uch like the baronial card, a **stock invitation** may or may not fold, may or may not print inside and out, and usually is **set in script**.

If the stock invitation is a flat card, create a new document (there is no template) the same size as the invitation with .25" – .5" (1p6 – 3p) margins, no facing pages, 1 column, and click on the automatic text box. Set text (or get text).

If the invitation is a vertical format that folds, the new document size will be the outside dimensions of the card when folded (not flat), .25" – .5" (1p6 – 3p) margins, facing pages on, 1 column, and automatic text box on.

Insert 2 pages after page 1 (3 if there is text on the **outside back panel** of the invitation), set text (or get text) and print with the spreads **button** clicked on.

A horizontal format should be set with no facing pages and insert 2 pages after page 1 (3 if there is text on the outside back panel of the invitation). Set text (or get text) and print without the spreads button clicked on.

> **Note:** When using **script typefaces** you may notice that the text size appears to be much smaller than the same **point size** in a **roman** type style. This is due to the angle of the text and the extended **serifs**. Use a larger type size and a very generous leading. **Justified** vertical alignment will usually achieve the optimum results of an open "feel" that complements script typefaces, providing there is not too much text to comfortably fit within the text box.

Function	Menu Location	Keyboard Equivalent
Get Text	→ File → Get Text →	Command/E →
Insert (pages)	→ Page → Insert	
Leading	→ Style → Leading →	Command/Shift/E →
New	→ File → New	Command/N
Print	→ File → Print	Command/P →
Size	→ Style → Size →	Command/Shift/ \ →
Vertical (alignment)	→ Item → Modify → Alignment → Vertical	Command/M →

Section 4
Return To Sender

Chapter 8
Standard Envelopes

#10 Envelope with 1/4" margins

Template EPS-68

Document Size:
   9.5 X 4.125"

Finished Size:
   9.5 X 4.125"

Margins:

T: .25 (1p6)

B: .25 (1p6)

L: .25 (1p6)

R: .25 (1p6)

Facing Pages:
   no

Automatic
Text Box:
   yes

Columns:
   1

Gutter Width:

Ruler Guide Positions:

V:

H:

Crop/Trim Positions:

V:

H:

Fold Mark Positions:

V:

H:

Recommended
Text Inset:
   .25"
is built into margins. For less,
begin with desired amount in
margin fields.

EPS-68 6/13/92 11:00 AM Page 68

text box

A

registration
marks button

tandard **#10** envelopes (template EPS-68) are 9.5 X 4.125" and their margins should almost always be at least .25" (1p6), no facing pages, 1 column, and click on the automatic text box.

Set text (or get text) and add necessary graphics (get picture).

> **Note:** Some envelopes, especially those that **bleed**, are printed as a **converted** envelope. A converted envelope prints flat and then is **die cut** and folded during the **bindery process**, thus converted into a pocket. A converted envelope is generally more expensive because of this lengthy process.

> As with any document, any items that bleed on a converted envelope should extend off the edge of the document at least 1 pica. Always check with your printer before creating an envelope with a bleed.

> **Note:** A document that is created horizontally will be in the **landscape** format in the page setup menu. For a vertical document that was changed to a horizontal after opening (through the document setup dialog box) you will need to choose landscape in the page setup menu before selecting print (turn the registration marks **button** on).

Other **stock envelope sizes** are listed in Appendix 4 and you should create each new document size to match one of these dimensions with .25" (1p6) or greater margins.

Function	Menu Location	Keyboard Equivalent
Get Picture	→ File → Get Picture	Command/E
Get Text	→ File → Get Text	Command/E
Page Setup	→ File → Page Setup	Option/Command/P
Print	→ File → Print	Command/P →

Section 5
To The Letter

Chapter 9
Letterhead

Letterhead with 1/4" margins

Template LH-72

Document Size:
8.5 X 11"
or Letter

Finished Size:
8.5 X 11"

Margins:

T: .25" (1p6)

B: .25" (1p6)

L: .25" (1p6)

R: .25" (1p6)

Facing Pages:
no

Automatic
Text Box:
yes

Columns:
1

Gutter Width:

Ruler Guide Positions:

V:

H:

Crop/Trim Positions:

V:

H:

Fold Mark Positions:

V:

H:

Recommended
Text Inset:
.25"
built into margins.

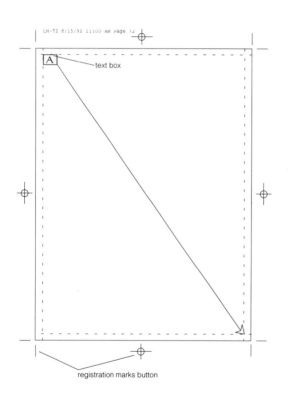

LH-72 6/13/92 11:00 AM Page 72

text box

registration marks button

Two standard sizes of **letterhead** are commonly used in the United States: letter (8.5 X 11") and **monarch** (7.25 X 10.5"). Each has its own matching envelope size, the #10 and the monarch.

Create a new document (or open LH-72) in one of the two sizes (click letter for 8.5 X 11), .25" (1p6) margins (less than .25" is not recommended, although many letterhead formats have much greater margins), no facing pages, 1 column, and enable the automatic text box.

Set text (or get text) and import graphics (get picture) as needed.

If the copy extends to the .25" margins, you will need to enlarge your print area because the letterhead is probably the same size as the maximum page size of your **desktop laser printer**. The **button** for reducing the **gripper area** is under the options button in the page setup **dialog box**.

Should any items bleed, extend them off the document edge by 1/4" (1p6) and click on the registration marks button when **proof printing** to ensure that the items bleed a sufficient distance for **trimming**. You will need to reduce the page or **tile the output** if your laser printer's image area is not larger than the size of the letterhead. (This will not change the size of the items — it will simply give you marks to proof bleed distances.)

Function	Menu Location	Keyboard Equivalent
Get Text	→ File → Get Text →	Command/E →
Get Picture	→ File → Get Picture →	Command/E →
New	→ File → New	Command/N
Open	→ File → Open →	Command/O →
Page Setup	→ File → Page Setup →	Option/Command/P
Print	→ File → Print	Command/P →

Those using a **service bureau** (and therefore, paying a per-page fee) may wish to **output** the envelope along with the matching letterhead.

In this case, open both the letterhead and the envelope documents; with the item tool select all elements in the envelope document, copy, and close the document.

Paste into the letterhead document and save as a different file name. Add **crop marks** as necessary to the outer edges of the envelope, keeping them at least 6pts from the actual edges of the envelope.

You can let the right portion of the envelope extend off the edge of the letterhead document and not affect the output. But this will not work on an envelope with items that bleed or even extend into the portion that hangs off the edge.

If the envelope, when pasted in, causes the text of the letterhead to move, select the text box containing the envelope and set the runaround to none. If it also contains graphic elements, set that runaround to none as well.

Function	Menu Location	Keyboard Equivalent
Close	→ File → Close	Command/W
Copy	→ Edit → Copy	Command/C
Open	→ File → Open →	Command/O →
Paste	→ Edit → Paste	Command/V
Runaround	→ Item → Runaround → None	Command/T → None
Save As	→ File → Save As →	Command/Option/S →
Select All	→ Edit → Select All	Command/A
Text Inset	→ Item → Modify → Text Inset →	Command/M →

Shortcut/Options:

If the envelope is a single text box, activate the text box and frame the text box with a .25pt (hairline) frame. The printer will use this frame to position the envelope correctly either on a **negative** or a **paper plate** then **opaque** the frame. It is not necessary to delete this frame once printed, nor is it necessary to also draw individual corner crop marks.

If the envelope contains several text boxes and graphic elements, you can achieve the same effect by drawing a text box 9.5 X 4.125", setting the runaround to none and dragging it over the envelope's items, positioning it correctly to indicate the margins.

Function	Menu Location	Keyboard Equivalent
Frame	→ Item → Frame →	Command/B →
Runaround	→ Item → Runaround → None	Command/T → None

Section 5
To the Letter

Chapter 10
Fliers

 ommon errors found in documents for printing are insufficient **gripper edge** on the **lead end** and incorrect **bleeds**.

I addressed the first error in Section 2, Chapter 1: Business Cards, and I've touched on it in each chapter since. **Presses**, **desktop laser printers**, photocopiers, and so on all require a gripper edge to pull the paper through its path. If you create a document that does not have a gripper edge, the pre-press department or printer will be forced to either reduce your document to allow gripper space or print it on an **oversized sheet**. Either way it usually means extra cost, which is passed on to you.

Don't try to guess the gripper amount. Talk with your print shop about quantity and quality requirements. In most cases the printer will assign a press and be able to dictate the gripper requirements.

Even documents that have bleed elements should adhere to gripper requirements. Don't place text any closer than .25" (1p6) to any **trim**, **fold**, **perforation**, or **die cut**. Though there are always exceptions to any rule, this basic guideline should keep your printer happy.

A bleed must physically extend off the edge of the document. It is not sufficient to simply stop at the edge. Most printers like a full .25" (1p6), but they usually won't resist .1667" (1 pica).

If you are using a **halftone** that bleeds, it is sometimes difficult to enlarge it to extend a full .25" in each direction. This, after all, adds .5" to both the width and height of the halftone and can be a sizeable difference.

A suitable alternative: Try adding a wide frame around the halftone in a black, white, or complementing color.

Adding a bar on just one edge as a graphic element can also help. Either of these (a frame or bar) must still extend off the edge of the document by .1667 – .25" (1p – 1p6). They may need to be as thick as 36pts to fully bleed and still frame the photo by enough to **trim**. See the examples below.

Talk with your printer about requirements for **bleed edges**. They may be willing to make concessions, depending on the final printed piece and their own in-house abilities/limitations.

In addition to using bleeds, fliers and data sheets may also print both sides.

Function	Menu Location	Keyboard Equivalent
Frame	→ Item → Frame →	Command/B →

Note: Any time a document prints on both sides, you should indicate how the reverse side **backs up**. (That is, whether the tops of both the back and front are at the top of the sheet or whether the top of the front and the bottom of the back are at the top of the sheet.) This is referred to as **head to head** or **head to toe**.

If the flier/data sheet folds, you may wish to create the new document larger, in order to accommodate hand-drawn **crop** or **fold marks**. The document should be .25" larger in each direction to allow for the crop marks you will add to indicate folds.

When you have manually drawn the crop marks, remember to turn off (that is, do not click on) registration marks in the print dialog box. While this **button** causes the **header** to print listing the file name, date, time, page, and tile position, it also adds (in this case, unwanted) crop marks outside the crop mark allowance area you have created.

Function	**Menu Location**	**Keyboard Equivalent**
New	→ File → New	Command/N

Section 5
To the Letter

Chapter 11
Resumés

RESUMÉ

Jane S. Doe
1111 Any Street
Anytown, Colorado 80000
(303) 555-1122

Personal
Objective
To secure a Sales and/or Marketing position with a company that rewards its successful employees with career growth and financial opportunities.

Work
Experience

Sales Representative
MRM Medical
Effective sales of medical equipment rental services, leases and purchases to hospital and health care institutions. Direct sales to hospital administrators, department heads, doctors and nurses. Successfully introduced new products. Increased sales from $40,000 to $80,000 per month. Instrumental in achieving a profitable branch. Three state territory. **Tied for top third office out of 105 offices in sales.**

Systems Coordinator
King Corporation
Marketing and sales of custom made mechanical equipment, instrumentation, control systems, and parts to municipalities, industries, consulting engineers and contractors. Project management to include purchasing, scheduling, client and vendor follow-up, and preparation of all technical manuals. Assist office equipment procurement. Involved in the hiring process and company training. Programming an C, III and Pascal.

Office Manager
Careers for Today
Corporate solicitation of executive positions. Accomplished successful searches for top industry talent and placement. Direct supervision and training.

Sales Representative
The Great Amusement Emporium
Sales of wholesale equipment and supplies to owners, distributors and manufacturers. Multi-state region. Two thousand accounts, four states.

Sales Representative
Colorado Aviation
Sales of single and multi-engine piston aircraft. Industry research on larger aircraft. Advertising and sales strategies.

After-Hours Manager and Investment Counselor
Western Federal Savings — Denver, Colorado
Investment counselling and marketing for both the private and commercial sectors. Responsible for marketing and cash analysis reports. **Designated manager of employees.**

Education
Red Rocks Community College — Computer Programming
University of Colorado at Denver — Engineering

Interests
Skiing, photography, cooking, nutrition, fitness and gardening.

References
Furnished upon request.

Next to **letterhead**, **resumés** are probably one of the simplest documents to create. In the U.S., they almost always are 8.5 X 11", have .25" (1p6) or larger margins, seldom **bleed**, and don't need to **work around a fold**. And as such, to print complete, a resumé need only have registration marks added with the **button** in the print **dialog box**.

The one difficulty that my clients have with resumés are tabs. How do you get a **subhead** to align with **indented text** without creating a bazillion text boxes? See the illustration on the previous page.

Create a new **letter-sized** document (no template has been provided), .25" (1p6) or larger margins, no facing pages, 1 column, and click on the automatic text box.

Set all text (or get text), dictate the size and leading. Be sure to press the tab key between subheads and corresponding text even though you have not yet begun to **format** the text.

Select all with the content tool, and, in the paragraph formats dialog box, enter a value in the left indent field. I have used 8p. This measurement must be wider than the longest subhead. (In the illustration it is the word "experience.")

In the first line indent field, enter the same value but as a negative (for example, left: 8p, first line: -8p). Click apply, and make sure that the body copy is wider than the subheads.

Function	Menu Location	Keyboard Equivalent
Formats	→ Style → Formats →	Command/Shift/F →
Get Text	→ File → Get Text →	Command/E
Leading	→ Style → Leading →	Command/Shift/E →
New	→ File → New	Command/N
Print	→ File → Print	Command/P →
Select All	→ Edit → Select All	Command/A
Size	→ Style → Size →	Command/Shift/ \ →

Holding the selection or select all with the content tool, go to the tabs dialog box and place a left tab at the same increment (8p) and apply to check for accuracy. Click OK.

As you can see in the "personal objective" line of the illustration, when there's two or more lines in a subhead, the subhead text can **float** above the paragraph text.

If you prefer that the first line of the subhead align with the first line of the body copy (as in the " experience" line), proceed as outlined above, typing only the first line of each subhead.

When finished, continue to format the indents and tabs as described. Then, insert the cursor at the end of the first line of body copy with a subhead that has a second line of text and insert a shift-return; then type the second line of the subhead and press tab.

Repeat this process with the second line of body copy if the subhead has three lines.

> **Note:** If you need to reformat the text after completing this process, watch the inserted shift-returns and subheads — they may move. I find it easier to delete the second (and third, etc.) line(s) of the subhead AND the shift-return (show invisibles) before I reformat.

Insert pages and link as necessary. Print, turning on the registration marks.

Function	Menu Location	Keyboard Equivalent
Formats	→ Style → Formats →	Command/Shift/F →
Insert (pages)	→ Page → Insert →	
Print	→ File → Print	Command/P
Select All	→ Edit → Select All	Command/A
Show Invisibles	→ View → Show Invisibles	Command/I
Tabs	→ Style → Tabs →	Command/Shift/T →

Section 5
To the Letter

Chapter 12
Certificates

Certificates (another easy one) have no real idiosyncrasies for printing. But they never seem to print! Each of my clients at one time or another has called about difficulty with printing not necessarily a certificate but a **certificate-type frame** on a **laser printer**.

One client left the document to print overnight and came in the next morning only to find the laser printer still chugging away at the document. She cancelled the print command and called me.

To help you understand the problem, **launch** the QuarkXPress application Frame Editor.

Select any of the more elaborate frames; especially one of the bottom thick frames. Choose edit from the file menu.

As you can now see, this simple-looking frame is actually a complex **bitmapped** image that a **2mb RAM** laser printer just can't manage.

So, when creating a certificate, you must select a simpler frame or **output** to a printer with adequate RAM for handling such a complex image. See Section 13: Chapter 3: RAM.

Certificates generally have very thick frames: 24pts or larger. Text inset needs at least 1p or more space. Vertically align as desired.

Function	Menu Location	Keyboard Equivalent
Edit (in Frame Editor)	→ File → Edit →	
Text Inset	→ Item → Modify → Text Inset →	Command/M →
Vertical (alignment)	→ Item → Modify → Alignment → Vertical	Command/M →

If the preferences are set so that framing falls to the outside, you may find that the thick frame of the text box will run off the edge of the page. For this reason, framing should be set to inside.

Function	**Menu Location**	**Keyboard Equivalent**
Preferences	→ Edit → Preferences → General → Framing	Command/Y

Section 6
Do Not Fold, Spindle, or Mutilate

Chapter 13
Tri-Fold Brochures

Letter-size tri-fold, vertical-panels brochure, (net size)

Template TRI-92

Document Size:
  11 X 8.5"

Finished Size:
  11 X 8.5"

Margins:

T: 0

B: 0

L: 0

R: 0

Facing Pages:
  no

Automatic
Text Box:
  no

Columns:
  1

Gutter Width:

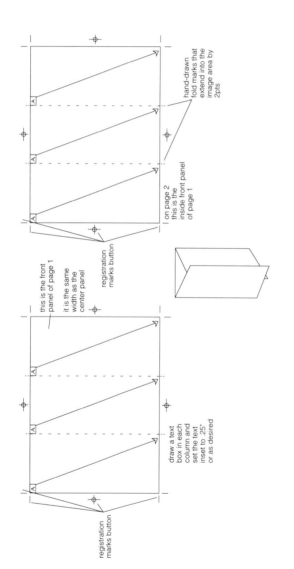

hand-drawn fold marks that extend into the image area by 2pts

on page 2 this is the inside front panel of page 1

registration marks button

this is the front panel of page 1

it is the same width as the center panel

draw a text box in each column and set the text inset to .25" or as desired

registration marks button

Ruler Guide Positions:
Outside (page 1)
V: 21p8
       43p10

Inside (page 2)
V: 22p2
       44p3

Crop/Trim Positions:

V:

H:

Fold Mark Positions:
Outside (page 1)
V: 21p8
       43p10

Inside (page 2)
V: 22p2
       44p3

Recommended
Text Inset:
       .25"

The illustration on the previous page shows a typical tri-fold brochure. The panel to be folded in is slightly (1/32 – 1/8" [2 – 4pts]) narrower so that it will tuck into the outside panel and not **buckle**.

This particular template/document is created **net size** with fold marks extending 2pts into the **image area**. Because QuarkXPress will not print any item that is solely on the **pasteboard**, you can force items to appear by pulling them slightly onto the image area.

The width of the panel that folds in will be determined by **paper weight**. A lighter paper requires a smaller width allowance than a heavier weight.

This allowance should not be created by trimming the panel narrower, though it often is when the designer does not allow for a narrower panel in the original artwork. Many times — especially during the **stripping process** — a print shop will be forced to adjust the panel width from the inside fold mark because key design elements would be affected by changing the position of the fold marks or by trimming the outside edge.

Template TRI-92 was created as a standard 11 X 8.5" new document, 0" (zero) margins, no facing pages, 1 column (using 3 columns gives 3 equal-width columns and would not allow for a narrower panel to fold in), and no automatic text box.

Function	**Menu Location**	**Keyboard Equivalent**
New	→ File → New	Command/N

Because the panels vary in width by 1/32", I find it easier to use **picas**. Change the vertical and horizontal ruler increments to picas in the preferences: general menu.

Insert 1 page after page 1 and, because page 1 will be the outside of the brochure, assume that the third panel will be the **outside front cover** and that panel one will fold underneath panel three.

Pull vertical ruler guides from the left ruler to 21p8 and 43p10. Draw text boxes to fit within these columns and set the text inset to a desired amount.

On page 2, you must reverse the panels: Panel three will be narrower (by the same amount as panel one on page 1) and panels one and two will be the same width. Pull ruler guides on page 2 to 22p2 and 44p3. Draw text boxes to fit the columns and set the text inset of each box.

Select your linking tool to link text boxes that have copy flowing from panel to panel. You may even link panel three on page 2 to panel one on page 1 if the copy flows from the inside of the brochure to the **outside back cover**.

Panel two of page 1 often contains text for a self-mailer, such as a return address or business reply mail information. Rotate all text -90° and drag into position within the page guides for that panel. You should stay at least 1p6 from all page guides marking that panel.

Type text (or get text) and import graphics (get picture) as required.

Function	Menu Location	Keyboard Equivalent
Get Picture	→ File → Get Picture →	Command/E →
Get Text	→ File → Get Text →	Command/E →
Insert (pages)	→ Page → Insert →	
Rotate	→ Item → Modify → Box Angle	Command/M →
Ruler Increments	→ Edit → Preferences → General → Vertical/Horizontal Measure	Command/Y →
Text Inset	→ Item → Modify → Text Inset	Command/M →

Position .25" (1p6) dashed vertical fold marks at the top and bottom of the page, aligning with the center two page guides. Begin 1p4 off the document edge and extend into the image area by 2pts.

Print with the registration marks button on and this will add the corner crop marks.

The portion of the fold marks that extends into the image area should either be **opaqued** by the **stripper**; or if **printed paper plate** should be **eradicated** by the press operator.

> **Note:** You must print to a printer with a sheet size greater than 8.5" width in order to pick up the fold marks — otherwise they will fall within the gripper area of the output device and will not print. If you must print to a letter-size printer, tiling the pages in the print **dialog box** will pick up these marks.

> Click on the ruler intersection in the upper-left corner of your document (rulers must be showing) and drag the intersection to .25" (1p6) above and to the left of the document edge. Print page 1 only, clicking on the tiling: manual button. Page setup should be in portrait format.

> After printing the first tile, again click on the ruler intersection and move its point to .25" (1p6) above and to the left of panel three on page 1. Print.

> Now the seam of your tiles falls between two panels and you will not incur the difficulty of aligning lines of text when taping the printed tiles together.

> Repeat the process for page 2.

Function	Menu Location	Keyboard Equivalent
Page Setup	→ File → Page Setup →	Shift/Option/P →
Print	→ File → Print	Command/P →

Tri-fold vertical panel, brochure with allowance for crops

Template TRI-96

Document Size:
    11.75 X 9.25"

Finished Size:
    11 X 8.5"

Margins:

T: 0

B: 0

L: 0

R: 0

Facing Pages:
    no

Automatic
Text Box:
    no

Columns:
    1

Gutter Width:

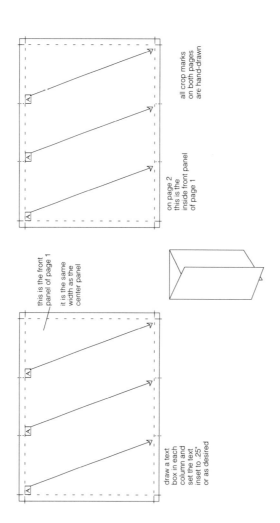

all crop marks
on both pages
are hand-drawn

on page 2
this is the
inside front panel
of page 1

this is the front
panel of page 1

it is the same
width as the
center panel

draw a text
box in each
column and
set the text
inset to .25"
or as desired

Ruler Guide Positions:
Both Pages
V: 2p3
        68p2
H: 2p1
        53p1
Page 1
V: 23p11
        46p1
Page 2
V: 24p5
        46p6

Crop/Trim Positions:
V: 2p3
        68p2
H: 2p1
        53p1

Fold Mark Positions:
Page 1
V: 23p11
        46p1

Page 2
V: 24p6
        46p6

Recommended
Text Inset:
        1p6

rop marks can be contained within the document but outside the text's **image area** by creating an **oversized document**.

Open template TRI-96 or begin a new 11.75 X 9.25" document, 0" (zero) margins, no facing pages, 1 column, and no automatic text box.

Change the ruler increments to **picas** and go to the master page.

Pull horizontal ruler guides to 2p1 and 53p1 and vertical ruler guides to 2p3 and 68p2. These page guides show the **outside trim edge** of an 11 X 8.5" sheet.

Add vertical and horizontal crop marks to each corner staying at least 6pts outside the margin guides. (See illustration on the opposite page.) Return to document view.

On page 1, pull two more vertical ruler guides to 23p11 and 46p1. Draw text boxes within these now-formed column guides. Change the text inset to a recommended 1p6. (Panel three of this page is the **outside front cover**.)

On the page guides marking the folds (the two center ruler guides), add dashed vertical fold marks 1p6 long. Stay at least 6pts above the top margin guide. Add fold marks at least 6pts below the bottom horizontal page guide and extend down 1p6.

Insert 1 page after page 1 and scroll/go to page 2. Pull vertical ruler guides to 24p5 and 46p6. Repeat the process of drawing text boxes, changing the text inset, and adding dashed fold marks.

Function	Menu Location	Keyboard Equivalent
Document	→ Page → Display → Document	
Go To... (page)	→ Page → Go To →	Command/J →
Insert	→ Page → Insert →	
Master Page	→ Page → Display → Master	
New	→ File → New	Command/N
Open	→ File → Open →	Command/O →
Ruler Increments	→ Edit → Preferences → General → Horizontal/Vertical Measure	Command/Y
Text Inset	→ Item → Modify → Text Inset →	Command/M →

Link together the text boxes according to copy flow. Set all text (or get text) and add graphics (get picture) as necessary.

Print the document with the registration marks **button** off and to a printer with a sheet size large enough to accommodate these marks.

You may also wish to tile the document to a smaller printer as discussed previously on page 95.

Function	Menu Location	Keyboard Equivalent
Get Text	→ File → Get Text →	Command/E →
Get Picture	→ File → Get Picture →	Command/E →
Print	→ File → Print	Command/P →

Section 6
Do Not Fold, Spindle, or Mutilate

Chapter 14
Half-Fold Brochures

Half-fold brochure, net size

Template HB-100
Document Size:
 11 X 8.5"
Finished Size:
 5.5 X 8.5"

Margins:
T: .25" (1p6)
B: .25" (1p6)
L: .25" (1p6)
R: .25" (1p6)

Facing Pages:
 no
Automatic
Text Box:
 no

Columns:
 2
Gutter Width:
 .5" (3p)

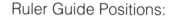

Ruler Guide Positions:

H:

V:

Crop/Trim Positions:

H:

V:

Fold Mark Positions:

H:

V:

Recommended
Text Inset:
 .25"
is built into the margins. To
change this, you must enter
different values there.

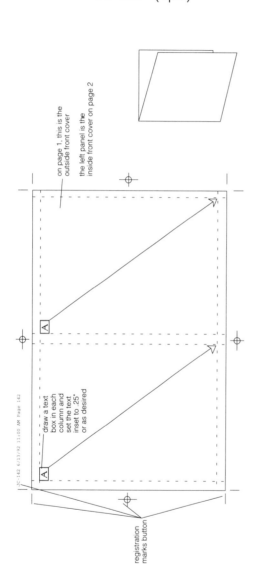

on page 1, this is the outside front cover

the left panel is the inside front cover on page 2

draw a text box in each column and set the text inset to .25" or as desired

JC-142 6/13/92 11:00 AM Page 142

registration marks button

 **alf-fold brochures** are quite easy. Open template HB-100 or a new 11 X 8.5" document, .25" (1p6) margins, no facing pages, 2 columns, and .5" (3p) gutter.

Draw two text boxes within these page guides.

Insert 1 page after page 1. Add text boxes between the column guides.

As with the **tri-fold brochure**, you may wish to link the text boxes to page 1 and cause text to flow from the inside of your brochure to the **outside back cover** (or from the front cover to the inside pages). Panel two of page 1 is the **outside front cover** and panel one is the outside back cover.

Set all text (or get text) and add graphics (get picture).

    Note: This is known as a **printer's spread** format.

Print with the registration marks **button** turned on; this will create sufficient crop marks. The center fold mark will be indicated by a registration dot (bullet). You can scratch this with an **X-Acto blade** to make it a dashed line, or, if you prefer, add vertical dashed fold marks at the center fold that extend into the document by at least 2pts.

Function	Menu Location	Keyboard Equivalent
Get Picture	→ File → Get Picture	Command/E
Get Text	→ File → Get Picture	Command/E
Insert	→ Page → Insert →	
New	→ File → New	Command/N
Open	→ File → Open →	Command/O →
Print	→ File → Print	Command/P →

Section 6
Do Not Fold, Spindle, or Mutilate

Chapter 15
Double-Fold Brochures

4-Panel, gate-fold 14 X 8.5" brochure

Template GF-104

Document Size:
14.5 X 9"

Finished Size:
14 X 8.5"

Margins:

T: .25" (1p6)

B: .25" (1p6)

L: .25" (1p6)

R: .25" (1p6)

Facing Pages:
no

Automatic
Text Box:
no

Columns:
1

Gutter Width:

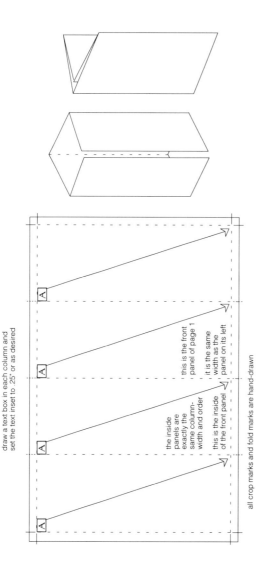

draw a text box in each column and
set the text inset to .25" or as desired

the inside
panels are
exactly the
same column-
width and order

this is the inside
of the front panel

this is the front
panel of page 1

it is the same
width as the
panel on its left

all crop marks and fold marks are hand-drawn

Ruler Guide Positions:

V: 3.72" (22p4)
7.25" (43p6)
10.78" (64p8)

H:

Crop/Trim Positions:

V: .25" (1p6)
14.25" (85p9)

H: .25" (1p6)
8.75" (52p6)

Fold Mark Positions:

V: 3.72" (22p4)
7.25" (43p6)
10.78" (64p8)

H:

Recommended
Text Inset:
.25" (1p6)

This four-panel, **gate-fold** 14.5 X 9" document is saved as template GF-104 (the final printed page will be 14 X 8.5") and has margins that are .25" (1p6) all edges, no facing pages, 1 column, and no automatic text box.

Upon opening, go immediately to the master page and drag vertical ruler guides to 3.72" (22p4), 7.25" (43p6), and 10.78" (64p8) to indicate the division between the panels.

These page guides now outline the four columns (panels). The outside panels are narrower so that they can fold in, and then in again without buckling. (See illustration on previous page).

Draw text boxes within these page guides and set text inset to a recommended .25" (1p6) or as desired.

Select the orthogonal line tool and draw .25" (1p6) vertical **fold marks** along the top and bottom edge at all three ruler guides separating the panels. Select all fold marks and use the measurements palette to choose a dashed line. Do not allow these fold marks to come within 6pts of the horizontal page guides at .25" (1p6) and 8.75" (52p6).

Function	Menu Location	Keyboard Equivalent
Text Inset	→ Item → Modify → Text Inset	Command/M →
Master Page	→ Page → Display → Master	

Select the orthogonal line tool again and, beginning 6pts off the document edge, draw the horizontal and vertical **crop marks** at each corner. Again, come no closer than 6pts to the .25" (1p6) margin guides. (See illustration on page 104.)

Revert to the document view and set all text (or get text) and graphics (get picture).

Insert 1 page after page 1.

Scroll or go to page 2 and set all text (or get text) and add graphics (get picture).

Panel three of page 1 is the **outside front cover** and panel two may contain text for a **self mailer**.

Rotate self-mailer items -90° and drag to the correct position within the page guides for that panel.

Print without the registration marks **button** enabled.

Function	Menu Location	Keyboard Equivalent
Document	→ Page → Display → Document	
Get Picture	→ File → Get Picture →	Command/E →
Get Text	→ File → Get Text →	Command/E →
Go To... (page)	→ Page → Go To... →	Command/J →
Insert (pages)	→ Page → Insert →	
Print	→ File → Print	Command/P
Rotate	→ Item → Modify → Box Angle →	Command/M →

Double-fold, 14 X 8.5" four-panel brochure

Template DF-108

Document Size:
14.5 X 9"

Finished Size:
14 X 8.5"

Margins:
T: .25" (1p6)
B: .25" (1p6)
L: .25" (1p6)
R: .25" (1p6)

Facing Pages:
no

Automatic
Text Box:
no

Columns:
1

Gutter Width:

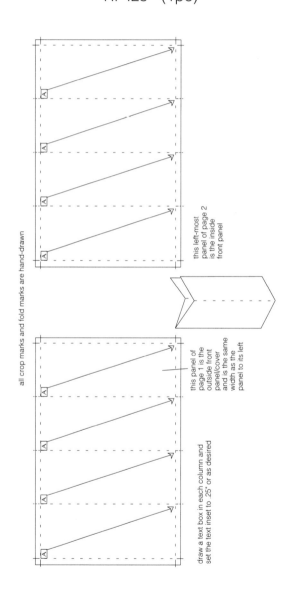

all crop marks and fold marks are hand-drawn

this left-most panel of page 2 is the inside front panel

this panel of page 1 is the outside front panel/cover and is the same width as the panel to its left

draw a text box in each column and set the text inset to .25" or as desired

Ruler Guide Positions:
Page 1 (outside)
V: 3.69"   (22p2)
       7.19"   (43p2)
     10.72" (64p4)

Page 2 (inside)
V: 3.78"   (22p8)
       7.31"   (43p10)
     10.81" (64p10)

Crop/Trim Positions:
V: .25"   (1p6)
    14.25" (85p6)

H: .25   (1p6)
   8.75" (52p6)

Fold Mark Positions:
Page 1 (outside)
V: 3.69"   (22p2)
       7.19"   (43p2)
     10.72" (64p4)

Page 2 (inside)
V: 3.78"   (22p8)
       7.31"   (43p10)
     10.81" (64p10)

Recommended
Text Inset:
.25" (1p6)

Double-fold brochures are folded in half and then half again as shown in the illustration on the previous page. This type of document is created in the same manner as a **gate-fold** except that the narrow panels are now the first and second panels of page 1 and the third and fourth panels of page 2.

Begin with a new 14.5 X 9" document (or open template DF-108) and margins that are .25" (1p6) all edges, no facing pages, 1 column, and no automatic text box.

Go to the master page and draw vertical and horizontal crop marks 6pts outside each corner as indicated in the illustration. The marks are .25" (1p6) and extend off the document edge by 6pts.

Return to the document view and on page 1, drag vertical ruler guides to 3.69" (22p2), 7.19" (43p2), and 10.72" (64p4) to indicate the division between the panels. These guidelines now outline the four columns (panels), with the first two panels approximately 2pts narrower. This is so that, when folded twice, they will not extend beyond the edge of the first fold (see illustration on previous page).

Draw text boxes within these guidelines and set text inset to .25" (1p6) or as desired. Set or get text and get pictures.

Function	Menu Location	Keyboard Equivalent
Document	→ Page → Display → Document	
Get Picture	→ File → Get Picture →	Command/E →
Get Text	→ File → Get Text →	Command/E →
Open	→ File → Open →	Command/O →
Master Page	→ Page → Display → Master	
New	→ File → New	Command/N
Text Inset	→ Item → Modify → Text Inset →	Command/M →

Select the orthogonal line tool and draw vertical, dashed **fold marks** along the top and bottom edge at the ruler guides separating the panels. Do not allow these fold marks to come within 6pts of the horizontal margin guides at .25" (1p6) and 8.75" (52p6).

Panel four of page 1 will contain the text and graphics for the **outside front cover** and panel three may hold text for a **self mailer**.

Rotate self-mailer items -90° and drag to the correct positions within the page guides for that panel. Stay at least .25" (1p6) away from the page guides showing the panel parameters.

Insert 1 page after page 1. Go to or scroll to page 2 and pull vertical ruler guides to 3.78" (22p8), 7.31" (43p10), and 10.81" (64p10). Draw text boxes with a .25" text inset within these page guides indicating the columns (panels).

Add .25" (1p6) dashed fold marks above and below the horizontal margin guides at .25" (1p6) and 8.75" (52p6). Stay at least 6pts from these guides.

Link the text boxes in the desired direction of copy flow. Set text (or get text) and get picture.

Print without the registration marks **button** enabled.

Function	Menu Location	Keyboard Equivalent
Get Picture	→ File → Get Picture →	Command/E →
Get Text	→ File → Get Text →	Command/E →
Go To... (page)	→ Page → Go To... →	Command/J →
Insert	→ Page → Insert →	Command/M →
Print	→ File → Print	Command/P
Rotate	→ Item → Modify → Box Angle →	Command/M →
Text Inset	→ Item → Modify → Text Inset →	Command/M →

Section 7
Better Than Butter (It's a Spread)

Chapter 16
Newsletters

4-page newsletter in a forced printer's spread format

Template NL-112

Document Size:
8.5 X 11"
or letter

Finished Size:
8.5 X 11"

Margins:

T: as desired

B: as desired

I: as desired

O: as desired

Facing Pages:
yes

Automatic
Text Box:
yes

Columns:
as desired

Gutter Width:
as desired

Ruler Guide Positions:

V:

H:

Crop/Trim Positions:

V:

H:

Fold Mark Positions:

V:

H:

Recommended
Text Inset:
none

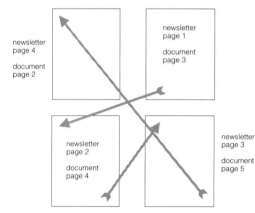

page 1 will contain no text

begin the outside front cover
on page 3 and link the
text boxes in the criss-cross
as shown

document
page 1

newsletter
page 1

document
page 3

newsletter
page 4

document
page 2

newsletter
page 2

document
page 4

newsletter
page 3

document
page 5

do not use automatic page numbering or jump boxes

Newsletters are not as difficult as as they may seem. However, **gripper edges** and **folds** are often ignored, and as a result, many newsletters have to be reduced to allow for a **gripper**, possibly throwing off the **fold**.

For a standard 8.5 X 11" four-page newsletter (printed on a 17 X 11" sheet and then folded in half) open template NL-112 or create a new 8.5 X 11" (**letter-sized**) document with .25" (1p6) (or more) margins, click on facing pages, columns as desired (usually 2 or 3), gutters as desired (2p for 2 columns and 1p6 for 3 are suggested) and click on the automatic text box if your text flows from column to column.

> **Note:** Stories placed separately around the pages are easier to lay out if you do not use the automatic text box and instead manually draw the required text boxes between the page guides.

If there are any repeated items on your pages, such as page numbers appearing in the same place or perhaps a horizontal **rule** running across the top of each page, switch to the master page and add the **common elements** there.

Revert back to the document view and delete all items on page 1.

Insert 4 pages after page 1.

Go to page 2 and choose section from the page menu. Click on the section start **button** and type "4" in the number field. Click OK. Go to page 3 and return to the section **dialog box**. Click on the section start button and make this page 1. Click OK.

Function	Menu Location	Keyboard Equivalent
Delete	→ Item → Delete	Command/K
Document	→ Page → Display → Document	
Go To…	→ Page → Go To →	Command/J →
Insert (pages)	→ Page → Insert →	
Master Page	→ Page → Display → Master	
New	→ File → New	Command/N
Open	→ File → Open →	Command/O →
Section	→ Page → Section →	

113

Complete all text (or get text) and graphics (get picture) with the **outside front cover** items on document page 3 (numbered page 1) and the **outside back cover** items on document page 2 (numbered page 4). See illustration on page 112.

It is okay to use automatic page numbering and automatic jump features with this forced printer's spread format.

Print the document with the spreads button checked and without the blank pages button checked. This will keep page 1 of the document from printing because it should be blank.

I change the center **vertical crops** (these are **registration dots** or **bullets**) to dashed lines (indicating a fold) by scraping them with an **X-Acto blade**.

> **Note:** This format would be used only if the document were being output to a **printer** that has an image area large enough to accommodate forced **printer's spreads**. If you intend to output the final pages to a printer with a maximum page size of 8.5 X 11", do not create the printer's spreads. (That is, page 1 of the newsletter is also page 1 of the QuarkXPress document, page 2 is page 2, and so on.)

Shortcut/Options:

Rather than using section, create a four-page document with facing pages turned on in the new dialog box and use an XTension such as Printer's Spreads ImPress, or InPosition to reorder the pages for direct output into printer's spreads.

Function	Menu Location	Keyboard Equivalent
Get Picture	→ File → Get Picture →	Command/E →
Get Text	→ File → Get Text →	Command/E →
Print	→ File → Print	Command/P →

Section 7
Better Than Butter (It's a Spread)

Chapter 17
Small Books

Booklet with automatic page numbering

Template SB-116

Document Size:
  5.5 X 8.5"

Finished Size:
  5.5 X 8.5"

Margins:

T: .5 (3p)

B: .5 (3p)

I: .5 (3p)

O: .5 (3p)

Facing Pages:
  yes

Automatic
Text Box:
  yes

Columns:
  1

Gutter Width:

document
page 1

document
page 2

document
page 3

document
page 4

Ruler Guide Positions:

V:

H:

Crop/Trim Positions:

V:

H:

Fold Mark Positions:

V:

H:

Recommended
Text Inset:
  none

SB-116 6/13/92 11:00 AM Page 116

A

a text box appears
here automatically
when you click on
the automatic text
box of the new page
dialog box

registration marks button

hen creating a **small book** or **pamphlet** you may wish to refer to Section 7: Chapter 1: Newsletters for additional information on **printer's spreads**. Small books may also closely resemble a **half-fold brochure**. See Section 6: Chapter 2: Half-Fold Brochures.

The most significant difference between a brochure and a small book may be the actual number of pages. A brochure is usually an 11 X 8.5" document printed both sides and folded, whereas a book will probably have many pages, and use **saddle stitch**, **perfect bind**, **GBC**, or some other binding method.

As in Chapter 1 of this section, whether or not you intend to use **automatic page numbering** will have a great impact on how you create this type of document. Two methods are described here and a template has been included for each.

For the first, I will assume that you intend to use automatic page numbering. In that case open template SB-116 or create a new document 5.5 X 8.5"; set all margins to .5" (3p); turn on facing pages and the automatic text box; and specify 1 column (or more if desired).

Function	**Menu Location**	**Keyboard Equivalent**
New	→ File → New	Command/N
Open	→ File → Open →	Command/O →

Note: Clicking on the facing pages **button** changes margins from left and right to inside and outside.

Note: The inside margin in this document can be made larger to allow for a binding method. Multiple-page documents can become difficult to read as text gets close to the **center binding**. On the other hand, many designers leave an extra wide margin on the outside of the page so there is plenty of room to "handle" the pages when turning them. Leaving wider margins is not always necessary and this document has not used either of these methods.

Go to the master page and add a text box for the page number. Inside this text box, hold down the command key and type a 3. You will notice that the text appears as: <#> and will remain so until a page is inserted while in the document view.

Format (character and/or format) the page number (<#>) as you wish the printed page numbers to appear. Select this text box and step and repeat; repeat count: 1, horizontal offset: 5.5" (33p), and vertical offset: 0 (zero).

Add all other graphics (get picture) or elements that are repeated (**common** to most or all pages) and revert back to the document view.

Shortcut/Options:

Use the show document layout palette to travel quickly from master pages to document pages by simply double clicking on the desired page or master page.

Function	Menu Location	Keyboard Equivalent
Character	→ Style → Character →	Command/D →
Document	→ Page → Display → Document	
Formats	→ Style → Formats →	Command/Shift/F →
Get Picture	→ File → Get Picture →	Command/E →
Master Page	→ Page → Display → Master	
Show Document Layout	→ View → Show Document Layout	

Set all text (or get text) and graphics (get picture). Insert pages as necessary.

Note: If you wish to insert automatically linked pages to your document via the insert pages dialog box, go to the master page and select the linking tool. Then click on the broken link symbol in the upper-left corner of the master page and then on the text box. Once back in the document view, insert your cursor in the text chain you wish to link to and the button for linking to the current text chain will be available in the insert pages dialog box.

Note: All **saddle-stitched** small books must contain a total page count evenly divisible by four. Because these pages will be printed **2-up** on both sides of an 11 X 8.5" sheet, you will need to add enough pages (whether blank or containing "fluff") to create a total number of pages evenly divisible by four.

If the book will be **wire-O**, **spiral**, or **GBC bound**, insert pages divisible by two. Odd-numbered totals must have an additional page inserted to bring the page count to an even sum. Pages may be added anywhere in the document: at the end of chapters, after the title page, or at the end of the book

Print the document, leaving the spreads button off and paste up or tape together the final output into printer's spreads.

Note: See next chapter for options in creating printer's spreads or refer to Chapter 1: Newsletters, of this section.

Note: Use an XTension such as ImPress, Printer's Spreads, or InPosition to output completed printer's spreads to an imagesetter.

Function	Menu Location	Keyboard Equivalent
Get Picture	→ File → Get Picture →	Command/E →
Get Text	→ File → Get Text →	Command/E →
Insert (pages)	→ Page → Insert →	
Show Document Layout	→ View → Show Document Layout	
Print	→ File → Print	Command/P
Master	→ Page → Display → Document	

Printer's spread small book, no automatic page numbering

Template SB-120

Document Size:
5.5 X 8.5"

Finished Size:
5.5 X 8.5"

Margins:

T: .5" (3p)

B: .5" (3p)

I: .5" (3p)

O: .5" (3p)

Facing Pages:
yes

Automatic
Text Box:
yes

Columns:
1

Gutter Width:

page 1 will contain no text

begin the outside front cover
on page 3 and link the
text boxes in the criss-cross
as shown

what a mess, huh?

document
page 1

small book
page 8

document
page 2

small book
page 1

document
page 3

small book
page 2

document
page 4

small book
page 7

document
page 5

small book
page 6

document
page 6

small book
page 3

document
page 7

small book
page 4

document
page 8

small book
page 5

document
page 9

do not use automatic page numbering or jump boxes

Ruler Guide Positions:

V:

H:

Crop/Trim Positions:

V:

H:

Fold Mark Positions:

V:

H:

Recommended
Text Inset:
none

There is .5" margin built into the
page parameters.

he second template assumes that you will either have no page numbers, that you will not implement the **automatic page numbering** or **jump** features, or that you will set up a forced printer's spread.

Open template SB-120 or create a new document as an 5.5 X 8.5", .5" (3p) margins, click on facing pages, 1 column, and click on the automatic text box.

Upon opening, go to the master page and add all **common** elements. You may add a text box for page numbers, type in a number (that will be replaced with the correct page number once added to the document) and **format** — just remember not to use the automatic page numbering. Unless you create a forced printer's spread as described in the Shortcut on page 122.

Revert to document view. Insert the same number of pages as the entire book (insert eight pages for an eight-page book, for example).

The pages do not link in the common pattern (from left page to right) but instead link in a criss-cross manner. For this reason, when inserting pages, you should not click on the **button** to link to the active text chain.

> **Note:** For this format you must insert pages that gives a total page count divisible by four.

Function	Menu Location	Keyboard Equivalent
Get Text	→ File → Get Text →	Command/E →
Insert (pages)	→ Page → Insert →	
Master Page	→ Page → Display → Master	
New	→ File → New	Command/N
Open	→ File → Open →	Command/O →

Begin on page 3 and link the text boxes in a criss-cross as shown in the illustration on page 120. When you reach the center page, link back up in a criss-cross pattern opposite the downward link. End the link on the second document page. If you have already added text boxes for page numbers, complete the printer's spread linking, and type the correct page numbers into the text boxes of each page. (See the illustration.) For forced printer's spreads refer to the Shortcut below.

> **Note:** Linking and unlinking text boxes are very complex commands and can easily cause **system errors**. It is highly recommended that you save your document in between each of the procedures described above to minimize the risk of a **crash**, and to save as much work as possible should a crash occur.

Shortcut/Options:

If you plan to use this format and must include automatic page numbering and/or automatic jumps, you can force QuarkXPress into this function by making each page a section start. Go to the page menu and select section.

In an eight-page document, Page 1 of the document will be section start page 8. Page 2 of the document is a section start page 1, and so on following the pattern shown in the illustration omitting the first page.

If you have a document with more than 8 pages and you do not know which pages will face each other, discuss the job with your printer and ask for a small **dummy** of the job. The dummy will display the pages in a **signature** with page numbers that you can follow when numbering the section starts.

Function	Menu Location	Keyboard Equivalent
Get Text	→ File → Get Text →	Command/E →
Insert (pages)	→ Page → Insert →	
Section	→ Page → Section → Section Start →	

Section 8
Cut Me Deep

Chapter 18
Rack Cards

Rack Cards cut three up from an 11 X 8.5"

Template RC-124

Document Size:
11 X 8.5"

Finished Size:
3.8 X 8.5"

Margins:

T: .25 (1p6)

B: .25 (1p6)

L: .25 (1p6)

R: .25 (1p6)

Facing Pages:
no

Automatic
Text Box:
no

Columns:
3

Gutter Width:
.5" (3p)

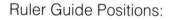

Ruler Guide Positions:

V:

H:

Crop/Trim Positions:

V:

H:

Fold Mark Positions:

V:

H:

Recommended
Text Inset:
none

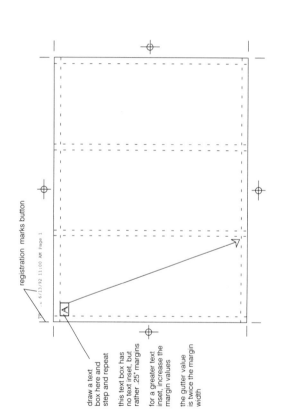

registration marks button

RC-124 - 6/13/92 11:00 AM Page 1

A

draw a text
box here and
step and repeat

this text box has
no text inset, but
rather .25" margins

for a greater text
inset, increase the
margin values

the gutter value
is twice the margin
width

ack cards vary in size but are usually one third of an 11 X 8.5" document and therefore easily produced.

Open template RC-124 or start a new document 11 X 8.5" (or three times the finished size width and height of your chosen format), .25" (1 p6) margins (or narrower if you prefer, though the **gutter** should always be twice the width of the margins), no facing pages, 3 columns, .5" (3p) gutter, and no automatic text box.

Draw a text box with no text inset within the first set of page guides.

Set text (or get text) and add graphics (get picture). Select all, step and repeat; repeat count: 2, horizontal offset: 22p, and vertical offset: 0 (zero).

If copy also appears on the back, insert 1 page after page 1 and repeat the process.

Print with the registration marks **button** on.

For **crop marks** between each panel, pull ruler guides to 22p and 44p. Add vertical crop marks above and below the document at these guidelines, beginning 2pts within the document and extending 1p4 into the pasteboard. Add these to the master page only if the document will be more than 1 page or prints on both sides.

Function	Menu Location	Keyboard Equivalent
Get Picture	→ File → Get Picture →	Command/E →
Get Text	→ File → Get Text →	Command/E →
Insert	→ Page → Insert →	
New	→ File → New	Command/N
Open	→ File → Open →	Command/O →
Print	→ File → Print	Command/P →
Select All	→ Edit → Select All	Command/A
Step and Repeat	→ Item → Step and Repeat →	Command/Shift/D →
Text Inset	→ Item → Modify → Text Inset →	Command/M →

Section 8
Cut Me Deep

Chapter 19
2/4-Up Note/Message Pads

5.5 X 8.5" Notepads, 2-Up

Template NP-128
Document Size:
  11 X 8.5"
Finished Size:
  5.5 X 8.5"

Margins:
T: .25 (1p6)
B: .25 (1p6)
L: .25 (1p6)
R: .25 (1p6)

Facing Pages:
  no
Automatic
Text Box:
  no

Columns:
  2
Gutter Width:
  .5" (3p)

Ruler Guide Positions:

V:

H:

Crop/Trim Positions:

V:

H:

Fold Mark Positions:

V:

H:

Recommended
Text Inset:
  none

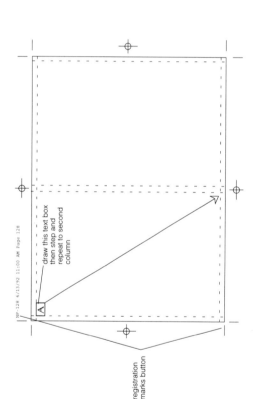

draw this text box then step and repeat to second column

NP-128 6/13/92 11:00 AM Page 128

A

registration marks button

**otepads** are easy 11 X 8.5" documents that are usually run **2-** or **4-up** and have a padded (glued) edge.

Begin a new 11 X 8.5" document (or open template NP-128), .25" margins, no facing pages, 2 columns, .5" (3p) gutter and no automatic text box. This makes for a 2-up format.

Draw a text box within the first set of column guides. No text inset, and set the text (or get text) and graphics (get picture).

Using the item tool, select all, and step and repeat; repeat count: 1, horizontal offset: 5.5" (33p), and vertical offset: 0 (zero).

Print with the registration marks **button** on. The center **registration dot** (**or bullet**) will indicate the center cut.

To request padding from your printer, dictate the edge to be padded, the number of sheets per pad, and whether or not you want to have a **chipboard** backing to each pad.

Function	Menu Location	Keyboard Equivalent
Get Picture	→ File → Get Picture →	Command/E →
Get Text	→ File → Get Text →	Command/E →
New	→ File → New	Command/N
Open	→ File → Open →	Command/O →
Print	→ File → Print	Command/P →
Select All	→ Edit → Select All	Command/A
Step and Repeat	→ Item → Step and Repeat →	Command/Shift/D →
Text Inset	→ Item → Modify → Text Inset →	Command/M →

4-Up phone message or notepads, vertical format

Template NP-130

Document Size:
8.5 X 11"

Finished Size:
4.25 X 5.5"

Margins:

T: 0

B: 0

L: 0

R: 0

Facing Pages:
no

Automatic
Text Box:
yes

Columns:
1

Gutter Width:

Ruler Guide Positions:

V:

H:

Crop/Trim Positions:

V:

H:

Fold Mark Positions:

V:

H:

Recommended
Text Inset:
.25" or as desired

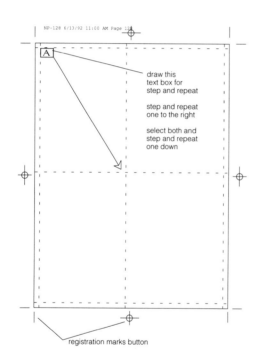

NP-128 6/13/92 11:00 AM Page 128

draw this
text box for
step and repeat

step and repeat
one to the right

select both and
step and repeat
one down

registration marks button

pen template NP-130 to create a **4-up** vertical document for **padding** (phone message pad, note pad, or a memo pad, for example).

Begin with a new 8.5 X 11" (letter) page or open template NP-130, 0" (zero) margins, no facing pages, 1 column, no gutter, and click on the automatic text box.

Activate the text box and double click on the W: **field** of the measurements palette, type in 4.25" (25p6), tab to the H: field and type in 5.5" (33p).

Set the text inset to .25" (1p6) or as desired.

Set all text (or get text) and graphics (get picture).

Using the item tool, select all, step and repeat; repeat count: 1, horizontal offset: 4.25" (25p6), and vertical offset: 0 (zero). Once again, select all, step and repeat; repeat count: 1, horizontal offset: 0 (zero), and vertical offset: 5.5" (33p).

If printing to an **output device** with a sheet size larger than 8.5 X 11", print with registration marks **button** clicked on. The center **registration dot** (**bullet**) will indicate the center cuts.

If your **desktop laser printer's** page limitation is 8.5 X 11" but the 4-up format is evident, the document will not need crop marks.

Function	Menu Location	Keyboard Equivalent
Get Picture	→ File → Get Picture →	Command/E →
Get Text	→ File → Get Text →	Command/E →
New	→ File → New	Command/N
Open	→ File → Open →	Command/O →
Print	→ File → Print	Command/P →
Select All	→ Edit → Select All	Command/A
Step and Repeat	→ Item → Step and Repeat →	Command/Shift/D →
Text Inset	→ Item → Modify → Text Inset →	Command/M →

Section 9
Sticky Situation

Chapter 20
Labels

ountless varieties of **pre-cut labels** are produced, some are output directly through a **laser printer**, others are made for **offset printing**. A large quantity or color would require that the label be printed via offset methods.

Regardless of what the label manufacturer claims, no laser printer manufacturer actually recommends (many, in fact, strongly protest) that label stock be run through the laser printer.

Because it is impossible to know the **stock labels** you will be using, I have instead listed the steps for creating the document. On this type of **pre-kiss-cut label**, it is not necessary to add any **crop marks**, as the text will print onto a label that will be lifted from a whole sheet. The outside-edge **registration marks** will be sufficient.

If you are creating a **custom label**, refer to Section 2, Chapter 3: Postcards, for help in setting up a document. Although it is unlikely that your label will match the size of one of the **postcard** formats described, that chapter may help you create the document.

To begin, create a new document the same size as the entire sheet of labels. Upon opening, change the unit of measure to **picas**.

Then, using a **pica ruler** (**pole**), measure from the top of the sheet to the top of the first label; add 1p (or whatever margin you choose) and type this measurement in the **field** for your top margin.

Function	**Menu Location**	**Keyboard Equivalent**
New	→ File → New	Command/N
Ruler Increments	→ Edit → Preferences → General → Horizontal/Vertical Measure	Command/Y →

Measure from the top of the sheet to the bottom of the first label (not to the top of the second label), subtract 1p (or desired margin) and this is the value for the bottom margin.

Measure from the left edge of the sheet to the left-most edge of the first label, add 1p (or desired margin) and type this value in the left-margin field.

Measure from the right-edge of the sheet to the right-most edge of the first label, add 1p (or desired margin) and put this value in the right-margin field, no facing pages, 1 column, and turn on the automatic text box.

Add text (or get text) and graphics (get picture) as desired.

Using the item tool, select all and step and repeat; repeat count: (specify how many across on the sheet), horizontal offset: (measure from the left edge of the first label [not sheet]) to the left edge of the label to its right), and vertical offset: 0 (zero).

Select all (item tool should still be selected) and step and repeat; repeat count: (specify how many down are on your pre-kiss-cut stock), horizontal offset: 0 (zero), and vertical offset: (measure from the top of the first label down to the top of the label directly below).

Print with the registration marks **button** turned on.

Function	Menu Location	Keyboard Equivalent
Get Picture	→ File → Get Picture →	Command/E →
Get Text	→ File → Get Text →	Command/E →
Print	→ File → Print	Command/P
Select All	→ Edit → Select All	Command/A
Step and Repeat	→ Item → Step and Repeat →	Command/Shift/D →

Section 10
Music to My Ears

Chapter 21
Cassette J-Cards

Jewel case insert (J-card) for a cassette, 2-Up and scored

Template JC-138

Document Size:
8.5 X 5.5"

Finished Size:
4 X 3.625"

Margins:

T: 5p6

B: 5p6

L: p9

R: p9

Facing Pages:
no

Automatic
Text Box:
no

Columns:
2

Gutter Width:
1p6

Ruler Guide Positions:

V:

H: 9p
12p

Crop/Trim Positions:

V: 1p
24p9
26p3
50p3

H: 5p6
27p6

Fold Mark Positions:

V:

H: 9p
12p

Recommended
Text Inset:
back flap: p3
spine: p3
front: p6

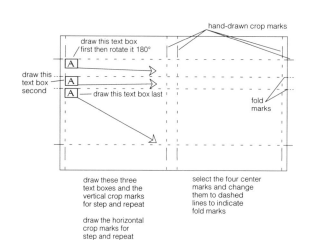

hand-drawn crop marks

draw this text box
first then rotate it 180°

draw this
text box
second

A

A

A — draw this text box last

fold
marks

draw these three
text boxes and the
vertical crop marks
for step and repeat

draw the horizontal
crop marks for
step and repeat

select the four center
marks and change
them to dashed
lines to indicate
fold marks

138

With most documents throughout this guide it has been important to include **gripper edge** for the **press**, **die cutting equipment**, and **bindery department**. The **J-Card** (the "cover" inserted into a cassette or CD case) is no exception. Keeping this in mind, these cards are created using an 8.5 X 11" sheet size which also is a **standard cut** and therefore, cuts evenly out of larger sheets.

> **Note:** Due to minute measurements, I use **picas** and **points** to create this document. Change the ruler increments in the preferences: general **dialog box**.

Open template JC-138 or a new 8.5 X 5.5" document with 5p6 top and bottom margins, p9 left and right margins, no facing pages, 2 columns, 1p6 gutters, and no automatic text box.

Pull horizontal ruler guides to 9p and 12p. Draw a text box with a p3 text inset to fit within the first set of page guides in the left column. See illustration.

Insert the cursor into this text box and type: "A _____" , press return and type: "B _____" (or whatever text is desired on this **back flap**). (The lines should extend to the right edge of the text box.) Format the text and vertical alignment as desired. With the item tool, select and rotate this text box, or these items, if you have imported graphics (get picture), 180° in the measurements palette.

Draw a second text box within the next set of guides (see illustration). **Set** text with a text inset of p3. (This area is the **spine.**) Add graphics and text.

Function	Menu Location	Keyboard Equivalent
Alignment (vertical)	→ Item→ Modify → Alignment →	Command/M →
Get Text	→ File → Get Text	Command/E
New	→ File → New	Command/N
Open	→ File → Open	Command/O
Rotate	→ Item → Modify → Box Angle	Command/M →
Ruler Increments	→ Edit → Preferences → General → Horizontal/Vertical Measure	Command/Y
Text Inset	→ Item → Modify → Text Inset	Command/M →

Draw a third text box with a text inset of p6 within the bottom set of page guides in the left column. Set text, add graphics.

Align on the p9 vertical margin guide staying at least 6pts above and 6pts below the top and bottom margin guides. Draw .25" (1p6) vertical crop marks. Select both marks and step and repeat; repeat count: 1, horizontal offset: 24p, and vertical offset: 0p (zero).

Select all with the item tool and step and repeat; repeat count: 1, horizontal offset: 25p6, and vertical offset: 0p (zero).

Align on the top horizontal margin guide and draw a horizontal .25" (1p6) crop mark 6pts from the left margin guide and another 6pts from the right margin. Extend crop marks to the left and right off the edge of the document.

Select both marks and step and repeat; repeat count: 1, horizontal offset: 0p (zero), and vertical offset: 3p6. Step and repeat these new marks; repeat count: 1, horizontal offset: 0p (zero), and vertical offset: 3p. And once more. Step and repeat the new marks; repeat count: 1, horizontal offset: 0p (zero), and vertical offset: 15p6.

Select the four center horizontal marks (two on each outside edge) and go to the modify dialog box and change them to dashed lines. These now indicate the **score** and **fold** between the back panel, the spine, and the front.

Print, clicking on the registration marks **button**.

Function	Menu Location	Keyboard Equivalent
Modify (lines)	→ Item → Modify → Style →	Command/M →
Print	→ File → Print	Command/P →
Select All	→ Edit → Select All	Command/A
Step and Repeat	→ Item → Step and Repeat →	Command/Shift/D →
Text Inset	→ Item → Modify → Text Inset →	Command/M →

Section 10
Music to My Ears

Chapter 22
CD J-Card

Jewel case insert (J-card) for a CD

Template JC-142

Document Size:
   9.5 X 4.75"

Finished Size:
   4.75 X 4.75"

Margins:

T: 0

B: 0

L: 0

R: 0

Facing Pages:
   no

Automatic
Text Box:
   no

Columns:
   1

Gutter Width:

Ruler Guide Positions:

V: 4.75"   (28p6)

H:

Crop/Trim Positions:

V:

H:

Fold Mark Positions:

V:

H:

Recommended
Text Inset:
   .25"

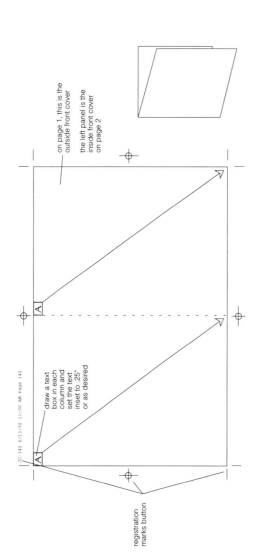

on page 1, this is the outside front cover

the left panel is the inside front cover on page 2

draw a text box in each column and set the text inset to .25" or as desired

JC-142 6/13/92 11:00 AM Page 142

registration marks button

A CD **J-card** can be created by opening template JC-142 or by beginning a new document 9.5 X 4.75", 0 (zero) margins all edges, no facing pages, 1 column, and no automatic text box.

Go to the master page and pull a vertical ruler guide to 4.75"(28p6). Draw a text box on each side of this ruler guide to fit and set the text inset as desired (.25" [1p6] is recommended).

Revert to document view and **set all text** (or get text) and graphics (get picture). Remember that the text box on the right is the **outside front cover** and the box on the left is the **outside back cover.** (This is a **printer's spread**.)

Insert 1 page after page 1. **Set all text** (or get text) appearing on the inside pages. Here, the box on the left is page 1 and the box on the right is page 2.

Print the document with the registration marks **button** on and, using an **X-Acto blade**, scratch the center **registration dots** (**bullets**) so that they appear to be a dashed line indicating the **fold/score.**

Function	Menu Location	Keyboard Equivalent
Document	→ Page → Display → Document	
Get Picture	→ File → Get Picture →	Command/E →
Get Text	→ File → Get Text →	Command/E →
Insert	→ Page → Insert →	
Master Page	→ Page → Display → Master Page	
New	→ File → New	Command/N
Open	→ File → Open →	Command/O →
Print	→ File → Print	Command/P →
Text Inset	→ Item → Modify → Text Inset	Command/M →

Section 11
A Divided Front

Chapter 23
Presentation Folders

9 X 12 Presentation Folder with a 4" pocket

Template PF-146

Document Size:
  19.25 X 16.5"

Finished Size:
  9 X 12" (folded)

Margins:

T: .25" (1p6)

B: .25" (1p6)

L: .25" (1p6)

R: .25" (1p6)

Facing Pages:
  no

Automatic
Text Box:
  no

Columns:
  2

Gutter Width:
  .5" (3p)

Ruler Guide Positions:

V: .625"   (3p9)
        .875"   (5p3)
        9.625"   (57p9)
        18.375"   (110p3)
        18.625"   (111p9)

H: .5"   (3p)
        12"   (72p)
        12.25"   (73p6)
        12.375"   (74p3)
        12.5"   (75p)
        16"   (96p)

Crop/Trim Positions:

V:

H:

Fold Mark Positions:

V: .625"   (3p9)
        9.625"   (57p9)
        18.625"   (111p9)

H: 12.25"   (73p6)

Recommended
Text Inset:
    none (.25" is built
into the document setup)

Labels on diagram (clockwise): ruler guide indicating the .25" text inset from the trim edge; margin guide indicating the width of the tab and score; ruler guide indicating the fold at the pocket; ruler guide indicating the bottom edge of the tab; center score and fold mark; the darker outline rule indicates the path to trace with the polygon frame tool and is used to make the die; margin guide indicating the top of the tab and pockets

Presentation folders, like most other documents, have many variations in size and style. The depth of the **pocket** can also vary and may have additional **die cuts** (business card slits and angled inside pocket edges, to name a few). A 9 X 12" pocket folder is probably the most common and therefore, the only template/set of instructions included here.

All presentation folders of this type are die cut. This particular document is a **standard die** at most **engraving services**.

This template also includes **tabs** for gluing the pocket to the folder at the outside edge. This process makes for a more expensive folder (especially because gluing is usually done by hand), but it is still very popular because papers can't fall out as easily if the folder is stored in a file folder in a cabinet.

Open template PF-146 or create a new document 19.25 X 16.5", .25" (1p6) all margins, no facing pages, 2 columns, .5" (3p) gutter, and no automatic text box.

Upon opening, pull vertical ruler guides out to .625" (3p9) and 18.625" (111p9). The area between these two narrow columns is for the die cut **tab**. This small strip will score and fold in toward the folder and be glued in place. This will ensure that pages do not fall out the sides of the folder.

Pull vertical ruler guides to .875" (5p3) and 18.375" (110p3) and horizontal ruler guides to .5" (3p), 12.25" (73p6), and 16" (96p).

Function	Menu Location	Keyboard Equivalent
New	→ File → New	Command/N
Open	→ File → Open →	Command/O →

These page guides now show the narrow columns for the tabs, the text area on the outside front and outside back cover with .25" (1p6) margin area, and the guideline where the pocket will fold up and be glued.

It is all right to allow items to **bleed** off into the .25" (21p6) margin area. Because this folder is die cut from a larger sheet, the bleed will be trimmed.

Pull an additional vertical ruler guide to 9.625" (57p9). This is the vertical fold; it intersects the horizontal ruler guide at 12.25" (73p6) (the fold for the pocket). Add .25" (1p6) dashed fold marks along these horizontal and vertical ruler guides. Stay at least 6pts outside the margin guides which are .25" (1p6) from each edge.

Pull another horizontal ruler guide to 12.375" (74p3). This is the bottom of the tab. At first glance you might believe this to be the top of the tab, but remember that the pocket will fold up at 12.5" (73p6), thus making this the bottom of the tab. The top of the tab is at 16.25" (99p9).

Rather than drawing crop marks in the corners, draw a polygon frame around the entire **outside trim edge** (refer closely to the illustration), including the jutting tabs (not along the fold ruler guide). This frame serves a dual purpose: First, it will be used by the stripper and then by the engraving service. The engraver will use this frame to make the die (if the printer does not already have one in this exact shape and size) for cutting the folder from the sheet.

Begin at the upper-left corner as shown in the illustration on page 146 and continue to outline the entire trim edge and tabs. When complete, frame the polygon in a .25pt (hairline) black or registration (color) frame.

Function	**Menu Location**	**Keyboard Equivalent**
Frame	→ Item → Frame →	Command/B →

Holding the polygon selection, send to back.

Pull a horizontal ruler guide to 12" (72p) (the bottom of the front of the folder) and draw text boxes within the inner sets of page guides. Set text (or get text) and get pictures.

If there is copy on the pockets, pull a horizontal ruler guide to 12.5" (73p6) and add text boxes here also. Drag-select all items on the left pocket and rotate 180°, then rotate all items on the right pocket.

> **Note:** Polygons are unpredictable and seem to cause **system errors**. Save your document often to reduce the chances of a loss from a **crash**.

Print without the registration marks **button** checked.

Function	Menu Location	Keyboard Equivalent
Get Picture	→ File → Get Picture →	Command/E →
Get Text	→ File → Get Text →	Command/E →
Print	→ File → Print	Command/P
Rotate	→ Item → Modify → Box Angle →	Command/M →
Save	→ File → Save	Command/S
Send to Back	→ Item → Send to Back	

Section 11
A Divided Front

Chapter 24
Tabbed Dividers

Cut or **tabs to a bank** refer to how many increments will divide the length of the sheet. A one-third cut indicates that the length will be divided into three equal sections; three to a bank means the same thing.

> **Note:** To differentiate between the QuarkXPress command set tab (style → tab) and a **divider** tab, the tab on the divider will be referred to as the segment.

Divider sheets can vary somewhat in size and depth of the segment, but a typical divider is 9 X 11" (or 11 X 9") with the segments extending an additional .5" (3p) past an 8.5 X 11" sheet. Sometimes a divider extends past the sheet size on three margins.

> **Note:** The size of the divider sheet is something you should discuss with your printer. This document is 11 X 8.5" because, even though a divider sheet may be cut to extend past a standard sheet of paper by a small amount on all edges, the area divided into tabs should match the sheet size being divided.

> **Note:** Because of the minute measurements all values are given in picas. You can change this in the preferences...general menu.

Function	**Menu Location**	**Keyboard Equivalent**
Ruler Increments	→ Edit → Preferences → General	Command/Y →

Divider Sheets with 1/2"-deep tab

Template: DS-152

Document Size:
  11 X 8.5"

Finished Size:
  11 X 8.5"

Margins:

T: 1p9

B: 1p9

L: 1p9

R: 1p9

Facing Pages:
  no

Automatic
Text Box:
  no

Columns:
  1

Gutter Width:

Ruler Guide Positions:

V: 2p3

H:

Crop/Trim Positions:

V:

H:

Fold Mark Positions:

V:

H:

Recommended
Text Inset:
    p3 each segment

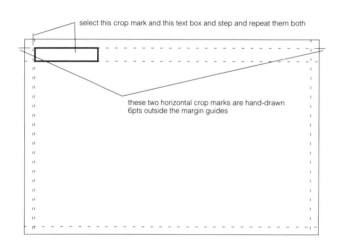

select this crop mark and this text box and step and repeat them both

these two horizontal crop marks are hand-drawn
6pts outside the margin guides

egin a new 11 X 8.5" document, 1p9 all margins, no facing pages, 1 column, and no automatic text box.

Using the orthogonal line tool, draw a .25" (1p6) vertical crop mark aligning on the 1p9 vertical margin guide. Extend the crop mark down to within 6pts of the horizontal margin guide at 1p9. Draw horizontal crop marks on the left and right margin edge, staying outside the margins at least 6pts.

Pull a vertical ruler guide to 2p3 and draw the first text box at this upper-left corner. Extend the box width to the measurement indicated in Appendix 5 and the height to 3p. (Or enter these two values in the W: and H: **fields** of the measurements palette.)

Format the text box with a type size, style, leading, alignment, vertical alignment, and text inset. Do not type in the text yet.

Use the item tool and select the text box and its vertical crop mark, step and repeat; repeat count: (number of segments per bank, less one since you have already drawn the first), horizontal offset: (refer to Appendix 5), and vertical offset: 0 (zero).

Select the last vertical crop mark and duplicate.

Step and repeat vertically the entire row and accompanying crop marks as necessary to give enough segments for the job you are creating.

Function	Menu Location	Keyboard Equivalent
Alignment (horizontal)	→ Style → Alignment →	Command/Shift/R, J, L, or C
Alignment (vertical)	→ Item → Modify → Alignment → Vertical	Command/M →
Duplicate	→ Item → Duplicate	Command/D
Leading	→ Style → Leading →	Command/E →
New	→ File → New	Command/N
Size	→ Style → Size →	Command/Shift/ \ →
Step and Repeat	→ Item → Step and Repeat →	Command/Option/D →
Text Inset	→ Item → Modify → Text Inset	Command/M →
Type Style	→ Style → Type Style →	Command/Shift/D →

Option-click on the link tool and link all text boxes of a row, beginning at the left and linking toward the right-most text box. It is all right to link down to the next row of boxes and across until you have created enough segments for all the divider sheets.

Activate the first text box and begin typing the text for the tabs. Use the enter key to jump forward to the next text box.

If you have any trouble getting the text to fit, select all with the content tool and reformat the text until it rewraps into its correct text box.

Function	**Menu Location**	**Keyboard Equivalent**
Select All	→ Edit → Select All	Command/A

The template DS-152 is for an 11 X 8.5" sheet and contains linked text boxes pre-formatted to center text both horizontally and vertically within each text box representing a segment.

> **Note:** In the template, all the tabs are in one document and in one row. It is all right to print the file in this manner. Most **pre-press departments** are aware that the tabs will print one per sheet and will separate the tabs during **stripping** or while **burning the plates**.

To use template DS-152, open the document, then insert the cursor into the first text box of the row you wish to use. (All other rows of text boxes and their corresponding crop marks may be deleted. The text box row and crop marks of choice can then be step and repeated vertically as necessary to provide enough segments.)

> **Note:** In the template, each text box has a set of corner crop marks and marks separating the individual segments. These marks show the sheet edge and division between segments and no other marks are needed.

Type text for all segments, using the enter key to jump from text box to text box.

To adjust type size, type style, or leading, it is easier to set all text first. If the text is set first and you then select all (with the content tool) and make adjustments to these parameters, you will be able to view in real time the effect your adjustments have on the fit of lines or groups of lines in a segment.

Function	Menu Location	Keyboard Equivalent
Delete	→ Item → Delete	Command/K
Leading	→ Style → Leading →	Command/E →
Select All	→ Edit → Select All	Command/A
Size	→ Style → Size →	Command/Shift/ \ →
Step and Repeat	→ Item → Step and Repeat →	Command/Option/D →
Type Style	→ Style → Type Style →	Command/Shift/D →

Note: Using the enter key may cause you to jump further ahead than you should. Just continue to type, then select all (with the content tool) and format the text size and leading until the type **re-wraps** into its proper segment.

Note: If you change the alignment to top or justified, it will be necessary to also indicate a first baseline offset. If you do not, the text will run to the edge of the die cut and could be trimmed off during the die cutting process. Also, if the vertical alignment is along the bottom, the text may run too close to the pages you are dividing and be impossible to read. A centered alignment with adjusted leading will be the simplest format.

Function	**Menu Location**	**Keyboard Equivalent**
First Baseline Offset	→ Item → Modify → First Baseline Offset →	Command/M→
Leading	→ Style → Leading →	Command/Shift/E →
Select All	→ Edit → Select All	Command/A
Size	→ Style → Size →	Command/Shift/ \ →

Section 12
Corralled Stock

Chapter 25
Preprints

Nearly all print shops use some type of **pre-print**. Whether in the form of business cards, brochures, envelopes, or any **long-run** with individualized messages, a pre-print can save a client thousands of dollars, months of time, and loads of effort.

To determine a job's feasibility for pre-print, most or all of the following requirements should apply:

1. The client will probably reorder within one year (or whatever amount of time you can afford to store the pre-printed **stock**);

2. The job has multiple colors;

3. The client will eventually use a large quantity (more than 5,000);

4. There would be considerable cost savings in purchasing the stock in larger quantities/sheet sizes; and

5. Parts of the job require an occasional plate or copy change.

As with the business card templates, letterhead, or envelopes, all elements of the document should be set as usual. Any elements of the document that are to be **imprinted** should be set in individual picture or text boxes, whichever applies. This will facilitate the **output** of both the pre-print and the **imprint**.

To output the pre-print portion of the document, create the document in its entirety (with imprint copy set in its own text or picture box as described above).

Once complete, select the items to be imprinted and suppress printout. Print the document or save as the pre-print version.

To output the portion that will imprint, select and suppress printout of the **base art** (pre-print portion) of the document. Save this document as the imprint, so you can edit it for future imprint revisions.

Function	Menu Location	Keyboard Equivalent
Print	→ File → Print	Command/P
Save	→ File → Save	Command/S
Save As	→ File → Save As →	Command/Shift/S →
Suppress Printout	→ Item → Modify → Suppress Printout	Command/M →

Section 13
A Plated Process

Chapter 26
Printing Processes

here are different methods for applying an image to a surface. In the print industry it may be by **offset**, **screen**, **gravure**, **flexography**, or **web**. However, each of these processes requires a plate or an original image of some sort.

In offset (the most common type of printing for small- to medium-sized print shops), the master image will either be metal or paper/polyester form.

The metal plate is a positive image of the job with one ink color per plate. This plate is made by exposing light through a set of **stripped up negative** images of the final art (called a flat).

Each plate can be exposed to an innumerable amount of flats. Some flats may contain only **crop marks**, a single **halftone** or color; others may only have **masks** for omitting items stripped to other flats.

Once exposed and processed a plate is wrapped around the plate cylinder of the offset printing press and passed by a set of ink rollers. The exposed areas of the plate collects ink and then in turn passes the ink off to another series of cylinders. The entire process is much like that of a rubber stamp that is inked and then pressed to paper.

The direct-to-plate method uses a polyester material that is exposed through a standard **imagesetter**. The cost is low per plate and because there is no paste-up, camera work, or stripping time, the overall cost savings can be substantial.

Like direct-to-plate, direct-to-press technology is new. This is a printing press driven by a PC. The PC front-end system instructs the press to make a plate, burning the images directly onto the printing plate using digital information from the PC file.

Some presses are equipped with the ability to print from plate material other than metal. These offset plates are generally made of paper or a type of polyester. The major difference in these types of plates compared to a metal plate is that they are imaged from positive art and not negative flats. Pages output from the Mac to high-resolution imagesetters or desktop laser printers are ideal for these lower-cost (and lower-quality) plates.

One other significant difference is that these plates are almost always used for **short runs**. Though the specifications on some of these types of plate material claim as many as 10,000 images, they are more often used for runs of 1,000 or less. These short-run plates are unacceptable for any job of more than one color, although they are not limited to black ink. The water solutions (fountain solution) used on the press may restrict certain presses from using this type of plate.

> **Note:** Three **XTensions**, Printer's Spreads, ImPress, and INposition, have the ability to reorder pages numbers and create **signatures** for direct-to-plate pre-press. Call XChange for more information.

Section 14
Gotta Get Ready

Chapter 27
Apple File Exchange®

Yes, you too can read a **DOS** disc. The manuals that were shipped with your Macintosh thoroughly explain the use of Apple File Exchange. But, since so many of us have purchased Macs second-hand, there is a need for a quick review of this file conversion utility.

To convert a file(s), launch Apple File Exchange. A directory of the contents of your hard disc will appear in the left window. Insert a DOS-formatted floppy disc into the **FDHD disc drive** and the files contained on this disc will appear in the window on the right.

> **Note:** The FDHD is the standard floppy disc drive for the Mac II family (except the original Mac II). It is also standard for the SE/30, the portable, and the laptop. Your SE may not, and your Plus does not, have this drive and therefore does not have the capabilities to read a DOS floppy.

Readable files are indicated by a **dog-eared page icon** with horizontal lines on it. Blank dog-eared pages probably cannot be recognized by Macintosh software and almost definitely not by QuarkXPress.

In the left window, choose a destination (a folder on your hard disc) for converted files and in the right window, select the files to convert. Once the file(s) are highlighted, click the translate **button**. When the translation process has stopped, quit.

The DOS disc will automatically eject from your computer and cannot be inserted and read unless you have already launched Apple File Exchange.

The translated text files can now be **imported** into your **word processor** program or directly into QuarkXPress. If the file does not appear in the window when importing (get text), it is likely that it was stored in a format unreadable by QuarkXPress. Try to import it into a word processor such as MacWrite® or Microsoft® Word and then resave it in a format that QuarkXPress can import.

To transfer documents to a pre-formatted DOS disc, launch Apple File Exchange, insert a DOS disc, select the file from the directory of your hard disc (the disc's name is listed below the window) and click the translate button.

The file should have already been saved in a format that the destination DOS computer will be able to read such as **ASCII** for text or perhaps **EPS** for graphics.

> **Note:** Three **XTensions**: WordPerfect DOS, Wang WP PC, and MS Word DOS, will eliminate the need to use Apple File Exchange. They read files originating in these DOS-based word processors while remaining in QuarkXPress.

Section 14
Gotta Get Ready

Chapter 28
Chooser/PostScript®

To print any document from a Macintosh, you should be familiar with the **Chooser**. It can be found under the **Apple menu** and is used to select **peripheral devices** such as printers, servers, and net modems.

The selected printer will have an effect on some of the **windows/dialog boxes** that appear in QuarkXPress — most importantly, page setup. For example, you would print a 9 X 12" document differently if outputting to a laser printer than to a larger-sheet-sized **imagesetter**.

If you should get an **error message** that indicates the Macintosh can't find the printer, go to the Chooser, click on the appropriate **icon** and select (in the window on the right) the desired printer. A printer name must be highlighted in this window to print a document.

When printing a document from QuarkXPress, be sure to adjust the settings in page setup. Page setup is the liaison between you and your chosen output device. You may need to indicate a **reduction** (to print oversized documents on the sheet size of your printer), a page direction (**portrait** or **landscape**), an **lpi**, a printer type (if using a high-resolution device, also paper width, gap, and offset), and behind the options **button**, items such as **invert image** and larger print area (.25" [1p6] grippers).

If you are using a **service bureau**, you may choose to save your documents in a PostScript© format. This might save re-runs due to missing graphics or **font address** incompatibility.

To save a document in this manner, page setup options must match the **output device** of the service bureau. If you call the service bureau to ask for preferred settings, the people there will be delighted.

If your Macintosh is running under System 7.x, there is a button in your print dialog box that can be checked (along with all other required buttons in this dialog box) to create a PostScript file for output. Click on all the necessary buttons, including PostScript, and click OK. You will be asked for a destination and a file name. Insert a floppy at this time and store directly to this disc for transporting to the service bureau if you're not sending your files via modem.

Under System 6.x, click on all applicable buttons in the print dialog box, then click OK and immediately hold down the command and the K keys at the same time. Hold until you get a message indicating that a PostScript file is being created.

This file will be named PostScript.x and is usually stored in the same folder as your QuarkXPress application (the destination may vary, so be aware) and can be drag-copied to a floppy disc for transportation.

You may rename the file but leave a **tag** such as ".ps" to the file name so that the service bureau will recognize it as a PostScript file.

Section 14
Gotta Get Ready

Chapter 29
RAM

y printer is slow." You don't have enough **RAM**.

"My document opens slowly." You don't have enough RAM.

"My document won't print." You don't have enough RAM.

"I can't open QuarkXPress." You don't have enough RAM.

"My document scrolls so slowly." You don't have enough RAM.

All these things are true — and more. Yes, RAM is definitely a necessary evil. You never have enough — but there is such a thing as sufficient, also known as, "just barely."

Two **megabytes** (2MB) of RAM is just barely enough to run QuarkXPress though if you're using **System 7.x** four megabytes (4MB) of RAM is the minimum. Eight for a half a bazillion fonts and 20 for a bazillion colors and a bazillion fonts.

Two megabytes of RAM in your **laser printer** is just barely enough, but 6 megabytes of RAM is heaven for a **monochrome system.**

System 7.x on a newer Macintosh enables the user to take advantage of **virtual memory**, which is a method for utilizing non-active hard disc space to double available RAM. However, virtual memory is considerably slower than RAM.

You still create the same size document (**K size**), as with less RAM. It only affects RAM-intensive functions such as running multiple applications, scrolling, printing, and so on.

So, in summary, can one ever have enough? Probably not, because when you do, the new and improved computers will surpass that need. Remember when we bought computers with 256K of memory and thought we had the technological world by the tail?

Section 14
Gotta Get Ready

Chapter 30
Disc Capacity

he last Macintosh-related thing you should be aware of is how much, or how little, disc space you need.

In a busy shop, 20 **megabytes** of hard-disc space will last about three days. After installing fonts, QuarkXPress, a few **XTensions**, a **word processor**, a **database**, and a **graphics program**, you'll have about two megabytes for storing created documents — if that.

I recommend 80 megabytes to my clients just getting into **DTP** — however, if it's an established shop with a medium-sized client base, I start there and go up.

A shop planning to produce 4-color process needs more — lots more. As in unlimited. Something along the lines of a removable cartridge. These cartridges can also be used to back up the internal hard disc, which should store all active jobs. Software and fonts don't usually need to be backed up each time since you have the original floppies.

Floppy discs come in two sizes — too small, 800 K (kilobytes), and 1.44 megabytes. The 800K are useful for storing or transporting client files but very often are just too small. A document must then be compressed or segmented and then unstuffed or rejoined for subsequent editing or printing.

Another option is compact discs (CDs). Though not yet nearly as popular as the removable cartridge, more and more **service bureaus** are using them. There is even a smaller version of the CD that has its own **disc drive**.

All discs have about the same failure rate — all drives do not. Some are definitely better than others. Ask, before you buy, who makes it, what kind of warranty, who fixes it, and how fast.

Appendix 1

Palettes

QuarkXPress and some of the XTensions used to enhance the application's abilities have window-type areas called palettes. Palettes have title bars at the top for moving the palette around on the screen; they also have close boxes for hiding them when you have finished. You may choose a tool from the tool palette, make minute adjustments to selected items with the measurements palette, or change a text's style with the style sheets palette. Other palettes include: color, trapping, and the library.

Whatever the need, the convenience offered by palettes have certainly been some of the most attractive features of QuarkXPress.

Tool Palette:

Item Tool: Enables the user to move items. Also to group, ungroup, cut, copy, and paste items. Used in some chapters to select multiple items by dragging a box to touch or encompass desired items.

Content Tool: When used inside a text box, it enables the user to type, import, edit, cut, and paste text.

When used inside a picture box, it enables the user to position, import, edit, cut, and paste graphics.

Rotation Tool: For rotating items manually (visually).

Zoom Tool: To reduce or enlarge the view or to select a specific area to be enlarged to fill the screen.

Text Box Tool: For drawing a box to contain text.

Rectangular Picture Box Tool: For drawing square or rectangular boxes to contain pictures/graphics.

Rounded-Corner Rectangle Picture Box Tool: For drawing boxes with rounded corners to contain pictures/graphics.

Oval Picture Box Tool: For drawing circular or oval boxes to contain pictures/graphics.

Polygon Picture Box Tool: For drawing picture boxes with three or more sides to contain pictures/graphics. Used in the presentation folder chapter to outline an odd-shaped die.

Orthogonal Line Tool: For drawing straight vertical or horizontal rules. Used in most chapters to draw the crop or fold marks.

Line Tool (Diagonal): For drawing straight diagonal lines.

Linking Tool: Used to create stories that flow from one text box to another.

Unlinking Tool: To break the flow of a story from one text box to another.

Appendix 2

Acceptable Postcard Parameters

The United States Postal Service has specific guidelines for mail that will be accepted at the postcard postage rate. (At this printing that rate is 19¢.) The guidelines include minimum and maximum size, weight, and in some instances, message.

Business reply mail (BRM) postcards must also follow these guidelines, and receive even more scrutiny on the front side. All items of the addressed side will be scanned by computers and therefore must be placed in precisely the correct position.

Minimum Postcard Size: 3.5 X 5"

Maximum Postcard Size: 4.5 X 6"

Minimum Postcard Thickness: .007"

Maximum Postcard Thickness: .25"

Postcard Postage Rate: 19¢

Message: Must be disseminating commercial information.

Personal messages will incur a first-class postage rate, which is 29¢ at the time of printing.

This information was provided by the Broomfield Colorado United States Post Office and is believed to be true and correct.

Appendix 3

Standard Baronial Card and Envelope Sizes

A baronial card is a standard-sized card, either flat or a fold-over, commonly used for announcements or invitations.

You will find the following sizes readily available from your printer or at some cash-and-carry paper suppliers. Other sizes are sometimes available from the manufacturer.

Size	Envelope	Sheet	Flat Short-fold Cards	Flat Long-fold Cards
A-2	4.375 X 5.75"	8.5 X 11"	4.25 X 11"	8.5 X 5.5"
A-6	4.75 X 6.5"	9.25 X 12.5"	5.625 X 12.5"	6.25 X 9"
A-7	5.25 X 7.25"	10 X 14"	5 X 14"	7 X 10"
A-8	5.5 X 8.125"	10.5 X 15.75"	5.25 X 15.75"	7.875 X 10.5"
A-10	6 X 9.5"	11.5 X 18.5"	5.75 X 18.5"	9.25 X 11.5"
A-Long	3.875 X 8.875"	7.25 X 17"	3.75 X 17.25"	8.625 X 7.5"

Appendix 4

Standard Stock Envelope Sizes

These standard sizes can be obtained from nearly every printer. As mentioned in the instructions in Section 4: Chapter 1: Envelopes, you should create your document the same size as listed here and include a text inset or margin guide of .25" (1p6) or more.

Number	Size
5	3.0625 X 5.5"
6 ¼	3.5 X 6"
6 ½	3.5 X 6.25"
6 ¾	3.625 X 6.5"
7	3.75 X 6.75"
Monarch	3.875 X 7.5"
8 ⅝	3.625 X 8.625"
9	3.875 X 8.875"
10	4.125 X 9.5"
11	4.5 X 10.375"
12	4.75 X 11"
14	5 X 11.5"

Window envelopes are created in the same manner as a standard envelope, but you must remember not to run your design over the area designated for the window. Here are the positions of the windows that can prevent you from making a sometimes costly error.

Number	Widow Size	Position From left	Position From Bottom
6 ¼	1.125 X 4.5"	.75"	.5"
6 ¾	1.125 X 4.5"	.875"	.5"
7	1.125 X 4.5	.875"	.5"
7 ¾	1.125 X 4.5"	.875"	.5"
8 ⅝ (or check)	1.125 X 4.5"	.75"	.8125"
8 ⅝ (or check) (small window)	1 X 3.75"	1.125"	.75"
Monarch (pointed flap)	1.125 X 4.5"	.875"	.5"
9	1.125 X 4.5"	.875"	.5"
10	1.125 X 4.5"	.875"	.5"
11	1.125 X 4.5"	.875"	.5"
12	1.125 X 4.5"	.875"	.5"
14	1.125 X 4.5"	.875"	.5"

Appendix 5

Tabbed Divider Tab Sizes

Though tabbed divider sheets may have varying depth segments, these segments are all .5"
(3p). You can easily change this measurement without affecting the page setup.

Cuts/Tabs To Bank	Text Box Width	Horizontal Offset
2	30p7	31p7
3	20p1	21p1
4	14p9	15p9
5	11p7	12p7
6	9p6	10p6
7	8p	9p
8	6p10	7p10
9	6p	7p
10	5p3	6p3
11	4p9	5p9
12	4p3	5p3

Note: The tabs vary in accuracy by 1 – 2pts in the overall width of the sheet, but will align properly if the stripper uses the crop marks included in the document.

Glossary

These listings may be open for interpretation.
Here they define the keywords and phrases as
they were used within the text of this guide.

#10
A standard measurement for an envelope. Also referred to as a business-size envelope.

1-up/2-up/4-up/6-up
Indicates how many duplicate items will print per sheet.

2MB
Two megabytes, or 2,048 kilobytes of random access memory. See RAM.

activate
In QuarkXPress, to make an item editable by clicking on it.

all caps
To type in all capital letters or to select and change text to all capital letters using that function of QuarkXPress.

Apple menu
A Macintosh operating system feature that contains items such as the Chooser, Control Panel, and desk accessories used for customization.

ASCII
Stands for American Standard Code for Information Interchange. A generic code representing alphanumeric characters that permits the exchange of text between operating systems. In QuarkXPress, these text files can be imported using the Get Text dialog box and exported within the Save Text dialog box.

automatic page numbering
Keystrokes that instruct QuarkXPress to insert the current page number, the page number from the previous text box in a chain, or the page number of the next text box in the active chain.

back flap
On a jewel-case cassette card (or J-card), the area shown when looking at the back of a cassette case.

backs up
How the reverse side of a printed piece will print in relationship to the front. See head-to-head and head-to-toe.

bar code
A series of bars, rules, or lines (such as a UPC or ZIP code) that are read by computerized scanners and relay information through the bars' placement, width, and size.

Baronial cards
A single sheet of card stock used primarily for announcements or invitations. Generally has a beveled edge.

base art
The portion of a design or image for printing to which all instructions, colors, and changes are labeled.

baseline
An invisible horizontal line on which letters sit. Lowercase letters such as "g" and "y" have descenders that hang below the baseline.

beveled edge
On a baronial card, the front out-side cover that has been depressed (embossed or blind embossed) 1/2" from the outside edge.

bindery person
One who performs the bindery operations in the printing process.

bindery (process)
Methods for finishing a printed job. Such as: cutting, padding, scoring, folding, die cutting, binding, and so on.

bitmapped
When a graphic image is formed by a matrix of dots or pixels rather than contiguous lines.

bleed(s)
Item(s) that extend beyond the image area or the trimmed edge of a printed piece.

bleed edges
The edges of a printed piece that have items extending past the trim.

body copy
Text that makes up the main portion of a printed piece.

buckling
The undesirable effect of folding a sheet of paper into three exactly equal sections without allowing for creep.

burning the plates
A photographic process in which the flats of negatives are exposed to thin sheets of plate material, usually metal. The material accepts the image, then is used as the master image for the printing press.

business reply mail postcard
A postcard with bar-coded information printed on it that instructs the postal service to return the postcard to the addressee. The addressee pays for return postage.

button
A small area within a window or dialog box to be clicked on with the mouse to dictate an action.

call it out
To write or type instructions next to a printer's mark.

center binding
The area at the center of two pages where they are bound.

center gutter
The white space dividing the inside columns of a page or of two facing pages.

center gutter trim
A cut made between two items to separate them or the area that will be cut away.

center mark
A pre-press mark made at the center of the sheet size on all four edges of the document.

center trim
A cut made between two items to separate them or the area between the two items. See center gutter trim.

certificate-type frame
A thick, decorative frame used on certificates.

certificates
A document usually defined by a thick, decorative frame.

chipboard
A cardboard backing glued (padded) to a short shift (stack) of sheets to form a sturdier pad.

Chooser
An item in the Macintosh's Apple menu that allows you to select printers, networks, and file servers.

commercially printed
Jobs that are printed on a larger press (not commonly found in a quick-print shop).

common
Items on a printed piece that appear on all versions, pages, or flats.

common elements
Text, graphics, or marks that appear on all printed pieces.

common marks
Crop, trim, fold, or perforation marks that appear on each page of a printed publication, and are stripped to a separate flat and burned onto each plate.

converted
An envelope design that is printed on a large, flat sheet and then die cut, folded, and glued to form an envelope.

crash
Jargon used when a computer freezes or fails to function.

creep
The process of compensating for the shifting position of the page in a saddle-stitch bind or a folded brochure.

crop
A cut made at an indicated mark. Also, the mark itself. See crop mark.

crop mark(s)
A mark that indicates to the bindery person that a trim or cut is to be made.

custom label
A self-sticking sheet of paper in a non-standard size or shape.

cut
A bindery procedure for trimming away excess paper or for separating items from a parent sheet.

cuts to a bank
The term for defining how many divider tabs will be cut per divider sheet.

database
An application for storing and organizing data or graphics.

desktop laser printer
A dry-process output device generally with a maximum sheet size of 8.5 X 14" and a lower resolution than an imagesetter. Resolution typically ranges from 300 to 1000 dots per inch.

dialog box
A boxed-in area that appears on a computer monitor in response to a command. It will ask for further direction. See window.

die
In this instance: A master image made of metal to "punch out" an odd-shaped cut.

die cut
To cut out an image using a die.

die cut edge
The portion of the image that falls close to the area where the die will punch.

die cut out
The process of punching or cutting an odd-shaped design from the sheet.

die cutter
The person or equipment that cuts an image from a sheet using a die.

die cutting equipment
The press used to cut an image from the sheet using a die.

disc drive (floppy)
A device accessed through the slot on the front of a computer, where a 3.5" disc is inserted so that data can be read or written.

divider tab
A portion of a divider sheet that extends beyond the edges of other sheets to indicate a division.

divider sheet
A sheet of paper that has a tab to indicate the division of pages or sections.

document/page
The electronic image of the sheet of paper or artwork shown on the computer screen

dog-eared page icon
A Macintosh symbol of a sheet of paper with a folded corner that indicates a page(s) of text.

DOS
Disk Operating System. Often used to refer to an IBM computer or compatible (clone).

double fold
Doubling paper over onto itself, twice. This creates four panels of similar widths.

drag-select
Using the item tool in QuarkXPress to draw a box around a group of items to select them simultaneously.

dropped in
Items that are burned onto the plate during the stripping process as opposed to those added before the stripping process.

DTP
Desktop Publishing. A term for the process of creating documents using personal computers rather than traditional methods.

dummy
A rough representation of a publication generally used to figure page positioning for stripping into flats and printer's spreads.

embossed
Using a die to impress an image into paper without the use of ink.

engraving services
A bindery company that is based primarily on the use of dies.

enter a tab
In QuarkXPress, to insert a tab character or set a tab on the tab ruler.

EPS
Encapsulated PostScript. A document file format jointly developed by Aldus, Adobe, and Altsys to facilitate the exchange of PostScript graphics files between applications.

eradicate
To erase unwanted images, dots, or small areas of text from a paper or electrostatic plate.

error message
A window that appears on computer screens indicating an erroneous command or request.

FDHD disc drive
A Macintosh floppy disc drive that is capable of accepting an MS-DOS-formatted disc.

field(s)
In database applications and other computer interfaces, an area designated for entering a value such as the measurements palette in QuarkXPress.

FIM
A postal bar code at the top of reply mail to be read by scanners.

final trim size
The finished size of a document when trimmed out from its sheet. A business card is 3.5" X 2".

finished size
The final trimmed size of a printed piece.

flexography
A type of printing that is characterized by the use of flexible, rubber or plastic plates.

floats
A line of text with a baseline that rises above other text lines.

format
To apply type style, size, and other characteristics to a selected area of text.

fold
To double paper over itself.

fold mark(s)
Dashed line(s) that indicate where a printed piece should be folded.

fold/score
A place indicated for a score and fold on a printed piece.

font address
A number assigned to a font used by the computer to identify it.

gatefold(ed)
To fold a sheet in half, then fold both outside edges into the center fold.

GBC (bound)
A book binding method originally developed by General Binding Company similar to spiral binding using plastic spines with fingers that fit into slots and encircle the pages.

graphics program
A computer application used primarily to create images rather than text.

cuts to a bank
The term for defining how many divider tabs will be cut per divider sheet.

gravure
A printing process in which minute depressions that form the image area are engraved or etched below the non-image area in the surface of the printing cylinder. Excess ink is scraped off by a blade and when paper comes into contact with the cylinder the paper absorbs the ink in the image area.

gripper, gripper area, gripper edge, gripper margin, or gripper space
The edge(s) of a sheet that the equipment holds to pull paper through its printing path.

grips
The act of holding the sheet to pull paper through its path to be imaged.

gutter(s)
The area of white space between columns or pages.

hairline
A line width (weight) equal to 1/4 point.

half-fold brochure
A single sheet of paper doubled over onto itself to attain four panels. (Two front and two back.)

halftone
The reproduction of continuous-tone artwork, such as a photo-graph, by screening the image into dots of various sizes.

head-to-head
A two-sided piece in which the tops of both sides are printed on the same end of the sheet of paper.

head-to-toe
A two-sided piece in which the top of the first side and the bottom of the back side are aligned.

header
When implementing the registration marks button in QuarkXPress, the line of text that appears stating the file name, date, time, page, and tile number.

heavy solid
A large, highly concentrated area of ink coverage on a printed piece.

high-resolution output
The film or paper product derived from an imagesetter or high-resolution printer.

high resolution printer(s)
An output device capable of printing with a resolution of 1,000 dots per inch or greater.

holding the selection
In QuarkXPress, keeping the item(s) selected through the next instruction.

horizontal format
A page or document that is wider than it is tall.

icon
A graphic symbol used on the Macintosh to represent files, applications, hard drives, and so on.

image area
The portion of a document that will appear on the final printed output.

imagesetter
A high-resolution laser printer (though not generally known as one) that images documents to a photo-sensitive material such as RC (resin-coated) paper or film for chemical processing.

import
To bring text or graphics into another application. In QuarkXPress: Get Text, Get Picture.

imprint(ed)
Text or images added to pre-printed material in increments as ordered by the client.

indented text
Text that is not flush with the rest of the text in an area.

inside back panel
The reverse side of the back panel or cover of a publication or multi-page brochure.

inside front panel
The reverse side of the front cover or panel of a publication or a multi-page brochure. Page two in most instances.

invert image
A function in the options button of QuarkXPress' Page Setup dialog box that causes the image to print in reverse.

J-card
Jewel-case insert. The card found lining a cassette or CD case with title and directory information.

jump
In QuarkXPress, to move forward in a group of linked text boxes. In a publication, to continue a story on another page or another area of the same page.

justified
Text that is evenly aligned along both right and left edges, as in newspaper columns.

K size
The size of a file measured in kilobytes.

keyboard equivalent
A keystroke or series of keystrokes that prompt QuarkXPress to complete a function that would otherwise be performed through a menu selection or dialog box.

landscape
A horizontally oriented page.

laser printer
An output device that uses a heat process to adhere small dots of toner to paper in order to form text and images.

launch
To start an application.

lead end
The edge of the sheet that travels through the path of a printer or press first.

letter-sized document
An 8.5 X 11" document.

letterhead
Stationery that has an individual's or company's name, logo, and address pre-printed.

line breaks
The ending of a line of text, or an indication of where it should end.

linked text boxes
A series of text boxes in QuarkXPress through which text flows.

long run
A print job with more than 10,000 pages. The Eagles, 1979. Glenn Frye.

lpi
Lines per inch. The screen frequency in a tinted (screened) area or a halftone. See halftone.

margin guides
Page guidelines whose placement is determined in the New page or Master Guides dialog boxes in QuarkXPress.

marks
See crop marks and fold marks.

masks
In offset lithography, an opaque material (generally orange - or ruby - colored) used to cover selected areas of a metal plate during exposure. Also used by production persons (both digitally and traditionally) to omit areas of artwork or to facilitate a trap between colors.

megabytes
1024 kilobytes. Used to indicate the capacity of hard discs, floppy discs, RAM, and so on.

metal plate
A flat, thin sheet of metal that is used as the master image on a printing press.

monarch
A 7.5 X 10" sheet of paper commonly used for letterhead.

monochrome (system)
A single color. Used to describe capabilities of monitors, video boards, and so on.

negative(s),negative images
A reverse image. Black areas appear as white and white areas appear as black. Also, clear film with reversed images that will be stripped into flats for burning metal printing plates.

net cut(s)
Items that cut apart with no extra space to separate them. Also called a butt cut. See TED (Turtle Exclusion Device).

net size
A document or sheet with no allowance (margin) for crop marks.

newsletters
A printed job that is characterized by the content. Usually inter-company news.

notepads
Sheets of paper padded (glued) at one edge for jotting notes and in this instance would include a chipboard backing.

offset
Lithography. The most widely used method of printing in which negatives are exposed to plate material, which is then treated with chemicals to cause the exposed areas to accept ink. The plate is then wrapped around a cylinder in the printing press and used as the master image. Paper passing through the path is pressed between another cylinder and a rubber-blanket-covered cylinder to receive the image.

opaque
To cover, conceal, or paint over when stripping to keep an image from burning onto the metal plate.

opaqued
A item that has been covered or concealed during the stripping process.

output
To print or the result of printing, usually from an imagesetter or laser printer. (Not as in offset.)

output device
A laser printer or imagesetter that outputs electronic files to paper or film.

outside back cover
The back sheet of a publication.

outside back panel
The back sheet of a brochure or card.

outside front cover
The front sheet of a publication.

outside trim edge
The outer edge of a document to be cut away (as opposed to a center trim).

oversized document
A document created larger than the trim size to accommodate items such as fold or crop marks outside the image area.

oversized sheet/page
A sheet of paper larger than the actual image area to accommodate items such as bleeds, crop marks, or color bars.

padded
Sheets of paper glued along one or more edges for the purpose of removing one sheet at a time, as in a notepad.

padding
The process of gluing sheets together for the purpose of removing one sheet at a time.

pamphlet
A brochure.

panel
A section of a brochure or pamphlet(s) separated from other sections by a fold.

paper plate
A master image used on an offset press made primarily of paper but may also include rubber or polyester.

paper weight
The density, thickness, or opacity of a sheet of paper. A heavy, obtrusive object to keep papers on your desk when it's windy.

parent sheet
The size of a sheet of paper as it is shipped from the mill. Generally larger than 20" square.

pasteboard
The area surrounding a QuarkXPress page in excess of the image area.

perfect
To offset print both sides of a sheet of paper during a single pass.

perfect bind
A process for binding publications that entails gluing all the pages together along one edge. The process is completed by wrapping the cover around the pages while the glue is still hot (wet). The resulting product is trimmed along the other three (non-glued) edges to complete a typical book.

perforation
A method for cutting paper in small, dashed increments to facilitate future removal of a section.

peripheral devices
External computer components that connect to the PC. Laser printers, image setters, scanners, and modems are peripheral devices.

pica ruler (pole)
A ruler divided into pica increments, used for measuring text, leading, columns, and so on.

picas
A typographic unit of measure equal to 1/6 of an inch.

plate
A thin, flat sheet of material that has been exposed photographic-ally to the artwork or negatives and then treated with chemicals so that ink will adhere to the exposed areas.

pocket
The area of a presentation folder that has been folded to the inside (and sometimes glued) to create a pouch.

point(s)
A unit of measure equal to 1/12 of a pica or approximately 1/72 of an inch.

point size
The height of a given character(s) of text.

portrait
A document that is taller than it is wide.

postcard(s)
A piece of mail that falls within a size range specified by the U.S. Postal Service.

postcard rate
The amount of postage required to mail a sheet of paper falling within postal guidelines for size.

PostScript
An industry-standard page description language from Adobe® Systems designed to handle the placement of text and graphics on a page.

pre-cut labels
Labels pre-cut to size.

pre-kiss-cut labels
Labels that are cut to a specific size and remain attached to their backing (so that they can be printed several at a time). See 2-up.

pre-press department(s)
The area of a print shop whose primary function is the generation of pre-press proofs, flats, and plates.

pre-print
Large amounts of printed stock that is stored and imprinted in smaller increments.

preferences
Default values (settings) for QuarkXPress or QuarkXPress documents.

pre-formatted
A floppy disc that has been prepared for reading and writing by a computer.

pre-scored
An impression made in paper before printing to facilitate a fold. See scored.

presentation folder(s)
A printed job that folds in half and may have pockets. Used for storing papers.

press
Machinery used to reproduce text and images onto sheets of paper in large numbers.

press proof, or press sheet
A finished printed sheet pulled directly from the press for the purposes of checking colors, positioning, and so on.

printed paper plate
Printed using a paper plate process that does not involve negatives, flats, or metal plates.

printer's spread(s)
The organization of pages according to how they will be printed as opposed to how they will appear in the final publication.

printer
A person who operates a printing press. A business who employs people who operate printing presses. Equipment that outputs text and images such as a laser printer or an imagesetter.

printing press(es)
See press.

proof
To read or check for errors in a document.

proof printing
To output in an inexpensive manner so that the document can be checked for errors.

quad-fold
A sheet of paper with three parallel folds, thus making four panels.

rack cards
A printed sheet that is used for display in a specially made rack.

Rapidograph pen

A fountain pen used by artists for traditional illustration purposes.

RAM
Random Access Memory. Internal computer memory for programs and data that may be altered. Information in RAM will be lost if it is not saved before the computer is turned off.

RC paper
A paper product coated with light-sensitive chemicals that is used inside of traditional typesetting equipment and imagesetters for receiving the image photographically.

real time
Computer operations that occur dynamically on screen.

reduction
A smaller version of an item or page.

registration dot, registration bullet, or registration mark
A circle with a horizontal and a vertical line that cross through its center. Used for aligning colors or layers of a design.

resumé
A document that lists the work and education history of a job applicant.

re-wrap(s)
The readjustment of the flow of text around an object on the page.

RIP (raster image processor)
A dedicated computer that converts images from a page-description language format to on-and-off dots to be recorded (printed) by the output device.

Rolodex cards
Small cards used for displaying phone numbers and addresses that fit onto a specially made holder.

roman
An upright (non-italicized) typeface.

rule
A line or bar. In QuarkXPress, you can draw a rule with the orthogonal and diagonal line tools or you can add rules above and below paragraphs in the Rules dialog box of the Style menu.

ruler guides
In QuarkXPress, guidelines pulled from the rulers (Show Rulers) to aid in aligning items on the document page.

saddle-stitch
A method for binding pages together. Pages are folded in half and stitched through the center gutter (fold).

scribing tool
A sharp, pen-like tool used to scratch the emulsion side of a negative.

script (text)
A typeface identified by its cursive slant, decorative descenders, and serifs. Letters might be linked as they are in longhand.

scored
An impression made in paper before to facilitate a fold. Scores can be made on the press during printing or as a function of the bindery process.

self mailer
A printed job containing information for mailing, such as return address, area for recipient's address, and the box outlining postage placement.

serif(s)
The small strokes at the end of the main strokes of letterforms. Times is an example of a serif typeface. Helvetica is a sans serif (without serifs).

service bureau
A company that will output client-created electronic documents at a high resolution.

set
Type (or typeset).

set a center tab
In QuarkXPress, place a tab marker on the tab ruler or press the tab key.

set all text
Type (or typeset) all body copy.

set in script
Type (or typeset) in a script typeface.

set the following text
Type (or typeset) the body copy that follows.

setting
The act of typing characters on a computer designed for typesetting.

several up
Many duplicate objects printed on a single sheet to be separated during the bindery process.

short runs
A small number of pages to be printed on an offset press. This number can be different depending on the press, its optimum speed, and other variables such as paper and ink colors.

signature
A parent, or large sheet of paper with several pages of a publication printed on it. The signature will be folded, bound, and trimmed to form a numerically correct section of a publication.

sinking
Dropping a line of text down from the top of the document, text box, or page.

small book
A book with a sheet size of 5.5 X 8.5".

spine
The center back of a perfect-bound book or J-card where the title is generally found.

spiral
A method of binding in which pages are punched and then a spiral-shaped wire is fed through the resulting holes.

standard cut
A paper size that is common to the industry or that cuts evenly out of a parent sheet.

standard die
A master image usually made of metal for printing, die cutting, or other bindery processes.

stepping all
To step and repeat (duplicate) all items.

stepping them down
To step and repeat (duplicate) all items down the page.

stock
Paper to be printed.

stock envelope sizes
Envelopes in standard sizes to be printed.

stock invitation
Blank cards that are to be imprinted with an invitation or announcement-like message.

stock labels
Pre-cut, self-stick paper to be printed.

stripped
Negative films placed into position in flats for the purpose of exposing (burning) the image onto a printing plate.

stripper
One who compiles negatives into flats.

stripping
The process of compiling negatives into position on flats for the purpose of exposing (burning) the image onto metal plates.

stripping process
See stripping.

subhead
A title line associated with a following block of text or a secondary line following the headline.

System 7.x
Versions 7.0 and above of the Macintosh Operating System.

system errors
A message that appears on a computer screen indicating a crash, or erroneous command or request.

tab(s)
An indicator mark for text alignment. An edge of a sheet of paper that extends beyond the width of the other sheet to show a division.

tabs to a bank
The number of segments a sheet is divided into for the purpose of showing separation between pages. See tab.

tag
The text line at the top of a page printed with the registration marks button activated that shows file name, date, time, page, and tile number. See header.

template(s)
A pre-formatted document that provides the structure, format, and/or layout for subsequent documents.

tile
A section of a printed page that fits together with other pieces of a document that is too large to be printed in its entirety on one sheet.

tile the output
An instruction indicating that you should turn on the tiling feature in the QuarkXPress Print dialog box.

traditionally
To create a document using industry-standard methods that were common before the advent of desktop publishing.

trim
A cut. To cut.

trimming
The process of cutting paper.

trim allowance
An area of the sheet reserved for cutting.

trim edge
The edge from which paper will be cut away.

trim mark
A short line indicating where a cut should be made.

trim size
The finished size of a printed sheet once the trims (cuts) have been made.

typefaces
A set of characters that share a distinctive and consistent design.

vertical crops
Marks that indicate a vertical trim or cut. See crop mark.

vertical format
A page or design that is taller than it is wide.

virtual memory
A process for utilizing non-active hard disc space as RAM. See RAM.

weight
The thickness (width) of a line. The density of paper.

window(s)
A boxed area on the computer screen containing a directory, message, or other information.

wire-O
A method of binding a book similar to both GBC and spiral. The pages are punched and joined together with a series of wire circles.

word processor
A software application for creating documents that are composed mainly of text rather that graphics and formatted pages.

work and tumble
A method of printing a two-sided document and using opposite ends of the sheet as gripper.

work and turn
A method of printing a two- sided document and using the same end of the sheet as gripper.

work around a fold
To set copy or graphics so as not to interfere with an intended fold.

XTension
A software addition that ties into QuarkXPress to modify or enhance its abilities.

X-Acto blade
A device with removable blades used for various cutting tasks.

Index

Each occurrence of a word throughout the book is listed here. For definitions, please refer to the glossary.

XTensions have been recommended in several chapters. They are software additions that enhance the capabilities of QuarkXPress. An XTension is easy to install. In most instances you just drag it into your QuarkXPress folder and restart QuarkXPress. Most commercial XTensions are distributed by:

XChange

P.O. Box 8899
Ft. Collins, CO 80525
800-788-7557
303-229-9773 FAX
For a catalogue, please call, FAX, or write your request.

BK Cynner Productions

This team of professionals works to bring desktop education to the publishing and printing industries. *Camera Ready with QuarkXPress* (formerly *QuarkXPress: Making the Most of Your Negative Experiences)* is one of the many products and services that we provide. On-site training, seminars and workshops, technical support, and video and audio training libraries for pre-press software and techniques are others.

For further information, contact:
Bill Klopfenstein
Director of Directions
BK Cynner Productions
P.O. Box 1726
Broomfield, CO 80038-1726
(303) 465-3891
(303) 465-6270 FAX

E-Scale/Business Reply Mail Guide

To receive a free clear-film guide (for checking placement of items on a business reply mail postcard) and E-scale (for measuring serif and sans serif type sizes, line widths, leadings, picas, and points), please send or FAX your request along to:

BK Cynner Productions
P.O. Box 1726
Broomfield, CO 80038-1726
(303) 465-3891
(303) 465-6270 FAX

NAME _____

ADDRESS _____

CITY _____

STATE _____

ZIP OR POSTAL CODE _____

COUNTRY _____

PHONE _____

FAX _____